SCARECROW STUDIES IN YOUNG ADULT LITERATURE

Series Editor: Patty Campbell

Scarecrow Studies in Young Adult Literature is intended to continue the body of critical writing established in Twayne's Young Adult Authors series and to expand it beyond single-author studies to explorations of genres, multicultural writing, and controversial issues in young adult (YA) reading. Many of the contributing authors of the series are among the leading scholars and critics of adolescent literature, and some are YA novelists themselves.

The series is shaped by its editor, Patty Campbell, who is a renowned authority in the field, with a forty-year background as critic, lecturer, librarian, and teacher of YA literature. Patty Campbell was the 2001 winner of the ALAN Award, given by the Assembly on Literature for Adolescents of the National Council of Teachers of English for distinguished contribution to YA literature. In 1989 she was the winner of the American Library Association's Grolier Award for distinguished service to young adults and reading.

1. *What's So Scary about R. L. Stine?* by Patrick Jones, 1998.
2. *Ann Rinaldi: Historian and Storyteller*, by Jeanne M. McGlinn, 2000.
3. *Norma Fox Mazer: A Writer's World*, by Arthea J. S. Reed, 2000.
4. *Exploding the Myths: The Truth about Teens and Reading*, by Marc Aronson, 2001.
5. *The Agony and the Eggplant: Daniel Pinkwater's Heroic Struggles in the Name of YA Literature*, by Walter Hogan, 2001.
6. *Caroline Cooney: Faith and Fiction*, by Pamela Sissi Carroll, 2001.
7. *Declarations of Independence: Empowered Girls in Young Adult Literature, 1990–2001*, by Joanne Brown and Nancy St. Clair, 2002.
8. *Lost Masterworks of Young Adult Literature*, by Connie S. Zitlow, 2002.

CAMPBELL'S SCOOP

Reflections on Young Adult Literature

Patty Campbell

Scarecrow Studies in Young Adult Literature, No. 38

THE SCARECROW PRESS, INC.
Lanham • Toronto • Plymouth, UK
2010

Published by Scarecrow Press, Inc.
A wholly owned subsidiary of The Rowman & Littlefield Publishing Group, Inc.
4501 Forbes Boulevard, Suite 200, Lanham, Maryland 20706
http://www.scarecrowpress.com

Estover Road, Plymouth PL6 7PY, United Kingdom

British Library Cataloguing in Publication Information Available

Library of Congress Cataloging-in-Publication Data

Campbell, Patricia J.
  Campbell's scoop : reflections on young adult literature / Patty Campbell.
    p. cm. — (Scarecrow studies in young adult literature ; no. 38)
  Includes index.
  ISBN 978-0-8108-7293-6 (cloth : alk. paper) — ISBN 978-0-8108-7294-3
(ebook)
  1. Young adult literature—History and criticism. 2. Young adults—Books and
reading. I. Title.
PN1009.A1C313 2010
809'.89282—dc22

                                                                    2009045563

∞ ™ The paper used in this publication meets the minimum requirements of
American National Standard for Information Sciences—Permanence of Paper
for Printed Library Materials, ANSI/NISO Z39.48-1992.

Printed in the United States of America

Contents

Foreword

Roger Sutton

I FIRST MET PATTY CAMPBELL IN 1980, when I was a student at the University of Chicago's Graduate Library School (or as YA services legend Dorothy Broderick called it, *The* Graduate Library School). With her colleague Don Reynolds, Patty had come to give a workshop at the Chicago Public Library, and young adult services coordinator Carla Hayden (now the director of Baltimore's Enoch Pratt Library, always a leader in YA services) had recruited some of us students to help out.

This for me was heaven and I felt like I was meeting a goddess. I was already an ardent fan of Patty's YA Perplex column in *Wilson Library Bulletin* and, more broadly, was a keen follower of what I thought of as the "California movement" led by such free spirits as Patty, Carol Starr, and Celeste West, who had edited the outrageous and inspiring *Revolting Librarians*, a manifesto for "liberated" librarians. Patty was their voice in young adult literature, advocating a freewheeling, free-reading approach to books and librarianship for teens. While her own taste in YA books was discerning, even elegant, Patty understood that teen readers needed books for all kinds of seasons and reasons, that car crash novels, comic books, and sex guides all held worthy places in the reading life of the young.

I met Patty as a student, continued to follow her work when I became a YA librarian, and went on to become a colleague cum competitor when I became YA columnist for *School Library Journal*.

(We once asked our respective editors if we could trade pages for a month. "No freaking way" was the immediate response.) While blood was never shed, there were battles between us—like the time I expressed serious reservations about *Beyond the Chocolate War* by her beloved Bob Cormier. But as time went on we found ourselves more and more often in the same boat, aesthetes in a sea of populism.

When I became editor of the *Horn Book* in 1996 and inherited Patty's "Sand in the Oyster" column from previous editor Anita Silvey, I could not have been more pleased. Anita had very smartly recruited Patty when *Wilson Library Bulletin* went under in 1995, recognizing that Patty's critical discrimination and sophisticated writing style were a great fit for the magazine. *Horn Book* reviewer Betty Carter once said to me that Patty knew better than almost anybody about how to put a sentence together, and it's true: Patty Campbell's literary voice is both unmistakable and immaculate. (I feel like I should say something here about her self-confidence, too. When I once complimented Patty on her fabulous legs, she replied, "Why do you think I wear such short skirts?")

She's an editor's dream, too. In the ten years I edited Patty she never missed a deadline, responded thoughtfully and efficiently to editorial queries, and only rarely tried to back a losing argument. Written by an open and inquisitive participant-observer, *Campbell's Scoop* is an enlightening survey of the first four decades of young adult literature. Dig in.

Roger Sutton
Editor in Chief
The Horn Book Magazine

Introduction

THE JOURNEY TO MATURITY OF YOUNG ADULT LITERATURE has been a long and bumpy ride, and I have been hanging on as a passenger for forty of the genre's forty-two years—as a librarian, an author, a speaker, a teacher, a columnist, but basically as a critic. During those years I have spent many words analyzing and reporting on the ongoing process of YA lit. For this book I have chosen a few of those writings that are still relevant to the development of the field, writings that I hope will be useful to young adult librarians and teachers who are immersed in the joyful endeavor of bringing kids and books together.

These words come primarily from two series of columns that I wrote for many years: a few from "The YA Perplex" of the *Wilson Library Bulletin*, and most from "The Sand in the Oyster" of *Horn Book* magazine. My first assignment for that literary journal was "Visiting Francesca," the long 1993 interview with Francesca Lia Block that appears near the end of this book. On the strength of that piece, then-editor Anita Silvey invited me to become a *Horn Book* columnist, and it was a productive association for fifteen years. For most of that time I had the good fortune to work with the fine editor-in-chief Roger Sutton and his other editors at *Horn Book*. Roger's guidance was demanding, inspiring, and only rarely infuriating, and he has made me a better writer.

My objective has always been to create a body of critical writing that would define young adult literature, identify its boundaries, trace its trends, point out its strengths and flaws, and celebrate its beauties. To set the stage for that endeavor, this book begins with three short histories of the field, one an irreverent personal memoir of my days as a librarian, one a more formal account, and one a tale of my editorship of two literary series that in themselves form a sort of who's who (and who *was* who) of YA lit. Further sections group columns around literary themes such as "Trends and Tendencies," "Defining YA," and "First Looks at Masterworks."

Other groupings reflect the concerns and interests of the genre as it has matured. I was fortunate enough to spot the beginnings of the graphic novel in the early eighties in France, long before it was accepted in the United States, and a visit to a Parisian comics store is recorded in the section labeled "The Dawn of Graphic Novels." No book about young adult literature would be complete without a tip of the hat (or a thumb of the nose) to the censor, and so I report on both national and international aspects in the "Censorship Near and Far" section. Comments on the influence of the American Library Association are drawn from my long association with that organization in the "Inside ALA" section.

There are several areas that have been particular preoccupations of mine. The spiritual dimension and its scarcity in YA lit has been a recurring subject for columns. My intense dislike for horror fiction sneaks in occasionally. A subject that generated fourteen columns in the early years (and many speaking engagements) was sex education, but not one of those columns in that changeable field is still relevant. And the great privilege of my life has been to be Robert Cormier's biographer. Two columns reflect that friendship, both written just after his death.

Throughout this book readers will also notice several pieces that record my insights and adventures during the twelve years when my husband and I spent nearly every autumn in Europe, researching first my book on street performers, *Passing the Hat*, and later our own how-to book, *Europe by Van and Motorhome*. I tried to keep these columns from abroad YA-relevant, but sometimes wandered off into wider speculation, as in the reflection on fiction and reality written at the foot of the Reichenbach Falls in Switzerland. And because young adult literature has been mixed with my life in a seamless sort of way, many of these pieces reflect that personal dimension. I apologize to those who would prefer a more formal presentation. But for those who join me in rejoicing over this great new body of literature and its fun, I say, "Welcome to a bowl of Campbell's Scoop!"

Part One

HOW WE GOT HERE

The Outsiders, Fat Freddy, and Me

A Librarian's Memoir

The following was originally presented as a speech to the Assembly on Adolescent Literature of the National Council of Teachers of English at the ALAN Workshop, November 22, 2002.

IT WAS THE END OF THE SIXTIES, and the times they were a-changing, and the social and political climate was exactly right for the birth of exciting new ideas and new literary forms for young people. It all began for me one fateful evening when I reluctantly went to the movies to see the Beatles in *A Hard Day's Night*. I went into that theater a nice middle-class housewife and came out a hippie.

A couple of years later I was a *divorced* hippie, with four teen-age kids, and I needed a job. I had a library degree, but I had used it for only two years, as a cataloger, a job I found so stupefyingly boring that I swore never to work in a library again. So I stayed home and raised kids, and later became an organizer with the civil rights movement. But now the wolf was at the door, so I applied to Los Angeles Public Library. They took one look at my skinny resume— "An organizer! You can do programs!"—overlooked my headband and bell bottoms, and hired me as a young adult librarian for the Westchester branch.

Originally published in "The Sand in the Oyster," *Horn Book* (March/April 2003): 177–83.

Libraries could afford to experiment during this period of prosperity. With the Library Services and Construction Act funds, for example, Los Angeles Public Library double-staffed its Venice branch, assigning two librarians to each position, one charged only with finding creative new ways to reach out to its very diverse public. With money from Title IIB of the Higher Education Act and funds from the Office of Economic Opportunity, libraries began to experiment with a wild range of options against a background of Vietnam War protests, the civil rights struggle, and the Age of Aquarius.

Programming was seen as the key. To the accompaniment of acid rock and Peter Max posters, library YA programs were a circus: speakers, panels, rap sessions, workshops, and exhibitions on comic book art, horror makeup, yoga, sharks, vegetarianism, astrology, karate, jeans decoration, ESP, filmmaking, amateur video and cable TV production, sex, drugs, and rock 'n' roll, plus a watermelon seed–spitting contest in the parking lot—anything that would bring teens to the library and get books into their hands. Actually, we didn't need to work that hard at it, because that influential population bulge, the baby boomers, were teens in those years, and they came pouring into the libraries.

YA library services rode the crest of this population wave with enthusiasm and federal funding. After *The Outsiders* hit the target and rang the bell, publishers were eager to fill this lucrative new market with more and more novels written in the new realistic style. We YA librarians were conscious of being at the crux of something important, as we banded together for support against the people we called "the old biddies" who ran our libraries—and our national association. As the youth culture became more and more alienated from mainstream America, we YA librarians felt ourselves to be a breed apart. This sense of identity coalesced around "The Young Adult Alternative Newsletter," a photocopied and stapled labor of love that was enthusiastically published by California librarian Carol Starr. In 1974, leading a revolution of us young Turks, Carol became president of the Young Adult Services Division of the American Library Association. Right away things changed. For example, ALA began to include YA novels in their highly influential "Best Books for Young Adults" list; whereas before "junior novels" had been specifically banned.

Librarians joyously celebrated the sense of developing a body of work at an American Library Association preconference in 1975 called "Book You!" (The title came from Carol Starr, who in her early days as a bookmobile librarian had often been annoyed by kids who would write the most common Anglo-Saxon expletive in the dust on her van, until she solved the problem by changing the *f* to a *b*, and closing the circles of the *u* and *c*, so that it cheerfully read *book you!*) At that preconference hundreds of YA librarians happily wrangled and schemed in small discussion groups to choose the best 100 books for young adults—a pattern the Young Adult Services Division of ALA, now the Young Adult Library Services Association, has repeated every few years since.

There was a tremendous sense of innovation, and we felt that we had just invented young adult services. Actually, libraries had been offering special services to teens for many years. The very first official young adult librarian was Mabel Williams, who in 1919 was appointed Supervisor of Work with Schools at the New York Public Library by the legendary Anne Carroll Moore, who wanted a way to ease "children" into the adult department after graduation. The first separate young adult room was dedicated in 1926 at the Cleveland Public Library. Other teen services were begun in 1927 at Los Angeles Public Library and in 1930 at Brooklyn Public. The first book about young adult literature was published in 1937—*The Public Library and the Adolescent* by E. Leyland—but it was mostly a cataloging scheme for collections in YA rooms. The earliest documented use of the term *young adult* for teen books is also 1937, although it didn't come into general use until 1958. And in 1933 the great Margaret Edwards was appointed to work with teens at Enoch Pratt Free Library in Baltimore.

But if there was no young adult literature before 1968, what books did librarians offer to teens? Actually, there *was* a subgenre of

fiction for teens, made up of simple school or adventure stories, but
as Edward Alm observed in a 1955 *English Journal* article, those junior novels were "superficial, often distorted, sometimes completely
false representations of adolescence," with stock characters, too-
easy solutions to problems, model heroes, saccharine sentiment,
inconsistent characterization, and representing the attainment of
maturity without development. Needless to say, these books were
not taken seriously. Mostly they were regarded as "transitional literature," useful primarily as bait for reluctant readers, which explains
why ALA kept them off the Best Books list for so long. Instead,
librarians scoured the adult shelves for books teens might accept,
and then promoted them aggressively in the library.

Margaret Edwards was especially passionate in her vision of the
librarian as a reading consultant and guide. At Enoch Pratt the goal
was "to introduce books to young people which will help them to
live with themselves as citizens of a democracy and to be at home
in the world." She believed that the librarian should work the floor
aggressively, approaching teens in the stacks with suggestions and
remembering what every single one had read before. The shining
goal was that each reader should be developed to his or her full potential. She articulated these articles of faith in her only book, *The
Fair Garden and the Swarm of Beasts,* written in 1969, seven years
after she retired.

When I arrived at the Los Angeles Public Library, Edwards's
book was presented to me as the holy bible of YA services, and I
was inspired by the example of Edwards's devotion to the cause but
heavily intimidated by her techniques, which I nevertheless put
into practice as best I could. (Many years later, in 1994, I got back
at her by serving as the editor of a new edition of *The Fair Garden*
and writing a foreword that pointed out several areas where she had
missed the boat.)

In the library, I was a devotee of the holy principle of face-out
shelving, lots of paperbacks on revolving racks, and messy boxes of
comic books, under my psychedelic Peter Max sign and the cascad-
ing greenery from a sweet potato plant in a Mason jar. *The Outsiders*

struck me as melodramatic and crudely written, but I was glad to have a book that kids pounced on as relevant. Teens loved Hinton and the other emerging YA authors, but they also had a litany of adult books that they used like passwords with one another and with me: *Stranger in a Strange Land* by Robert Heinlein; *Siddartha* and *Steppenwolf* by Hermann Hesse; *The Teachings of Don Juan* by Carlos Castenada.

And *The Lord of the Rings*, which utterly entranced the whole generation. We YA librarians had a trickle-down theory (not like Reagan's economic version) that held that reading fads and enthusiasms began on the college level and then worked their way down through a descending hierarchy of younger siblings to high school and then junior high. The passion for *Lord of the Rings* was an example; it began in 1965 with college kids when the American paperback edition appeared, but by the early seventies, teens were devouring it. All teens, even kids we had labeled nonreaders, worked their way through those three, big, fat, difficult books with a wild joy. (I get a distinct feeling of déjà vu from Pottermania.)

To put the enthusiasm for *Lord of the Rings* into perspective, it helps to know just how scarce fantasy was at the time and how this trilogy spurred its development. I chaired a committee in 1973 that set out to produce an annotated bibliography of 150 fantasy novels. We couldn't do it. Although we tried our best, we could only come up with a total of 147, even including ancient and obscure works like George Meredith's 1855 story, *The Shaving of Shagpat. Lord of the Rings* was unique in its time, although that's hard to remember now, when the pattern of heroic fantasy it established is so ubiquitous.

Then in 1971 *Go Ask Alice* hit the shelves and we found out what a monster popularity can be. This supposedly anonymous diary of a girl who descended into the drug culture and killed herself at the end generated all kinds of speculation and rumor, about how it arrived at the publisher's offices scribbled on brown paper bags, and how the author might be Art Linkletter's daughter, and so forth. All of which was a great spur to sales, of course. You all know, I'm sure, that the author was actually a woman named Beatrice Sparks, who is still doing very well with this anonymous business in many other books.

No matter how many trips we made to the paperback warehouse, there were never enough copies on the shelf. Ultimately, *Go Ask Alice* forced paperback publishers to recognize the economic power of the new genre in paperback, and we were off in the direction that was to lead to *Fear Street* and *Sweet Valley High*.

When in 1972 I became assistant to Young Adult Services Coordinator Mel Rosenberg, I got to help fight the sex education wars. The seventies were the height of the sexual revolution, and the specter of AIDS had not yet appeared to spoil the party. Much of young adult publishing was devoted to either trying to keep teens out of the water or teaching them to swim with the current. The "first-time" scene was almost obligatory in YA novels, and some of these passages were very graphic—and almost none of them mentioned contraception. Norma Klein, that great advocate of sexual freedom, was in her heyday, writing novel after novel. Sex education manuals were legion, in all styles and levels of audacity.

One that Mel Rosenberg and I found exquisitely amusing was *Facts o' Life Funnies*, a collection of sex ed comics by some of the leading artists of what were then known as "underground comics." Our favorite was "Fat Freddy Gets the Clap," in which the eponymous hero arrives at the free clinic with his enormously swollen male member swathed in bandages. The doctor, a large amiable woman, slaps him on the back and advises him heartily, "You gotta watch where you stick that thing, kid!"

This is probably the right time to explain that in the seventies many of us felt that our readers were high school kids, even college students. I booktalked only reluctantly to junior high classes, despite obvious evidence that this was our most receptive audience. We rejected as "too young" authors like Scott O'Dell and Katherine Paterson, and, following Margaret Edwards's lead, we shooed sixth and seventh graders away from the YA section and kept them out of our programs and discussion groups.

Most YA librarians today would admit that they are serving the sixth to ninth grades and losing the older readers. But a young adult literature aimed at older readers (even if only ostensibly) had its value. In the seventies, by focusing on the older teens and making their protagonists sixteen rather than fourteen, young adult authors were given a freedom to discuss touchy topics we are only just now regaining after the repressive eighties and early nineties.

Forever, of course, was the bombshell. Not so much because of the content—it was pretty graphic, but we had seen graphic before. No, the reason it caused a furor among teachers and librarians was that Judy Blume's audience up to that point had been comprised of little girls. Bradbury Press, although it published *Forever* as an adult book—with a double bed on the cover—left us with a horrendous selection problem; at the same time we recognized the novel's greatness. Was it a YA book or not? ALA voted in the negative by excluding it from the 1975 Best Books list. Teens, however, ignored us and read it avidly—and still do, in spite of its problems for the age of AIDS. But it is a misunderstanding to say that *Forever* freed authors to write about sex. The truth is that it did the opposite: its notoriety brought parents' attention to the free speaking that had been going on under their noses in books for teens, so that a wave of censorship challenges followed (not to speak of all the boys named Ralph who were motivated to beg their parents for a name change).

After AIDS there was a ten-year silence in YA books about things sexual, while everyone fretted about what to say to the young about sex, a puzzle that we have not yet completely solved.

But the seventies were a happier—and in a way a more innocent—time. We could go to YASD conferences on sex education materials and come back with official ALA T-shirts covered with cartoons of copulating couples (a T-shirt I wore for years, even to the grocery store), or we could arrive at work wearing another T-shirt that read "I am a young adulteress" and the boss wouldn't make us go home and change.

Finally, in 1974 all of this excitement and rich promise came to fulfillment with Robert Cormier's *The Chocolate War*. Oh, there had already been other YA books of lasting excellence—*A Hero Ain't Nothin' But a Sandwich, Slake's Limbo, House of Stairs, Deathwatch*. Other writers, from what was to become the YA canon, had already published first works: Richard Peck, Laurence Yep, M. E. Kerr, Harry Mazer, Norma Fox Mazer. But *The Chocolate War* was something else again—a book that shook us profoundly, a book that nobody could ignore. The critics went wild, some of them foaming at the mouth, others singing the book's praises extravagantly. Richard Peck said he wished he had written it. Betsy Hearne wrote a negative review in *Booklist* that was highlighted by a black mourning border. The universe of young adult publishing had been disturbed, and would be, forever after. And the door was opened for all the honest, fresh, stylistically daring, startling, terrifying, and wonderful fiction that has been our legacy ever since.

A (Not So) Short
History of YA Lit

THE RIVER OF YOUNG ADULT LITERATURE is overflowing its banks just now. From the trickle of a few books in the beginning almost forty years ago, it has grown to a mighty flood of fine writing. Fed by tributaries of new forms, new subjects, and passing trends, it has survived the drought of the nineties to become a major part of the watercourse of world literature. What are the trends the genre has grown through, and how does it differ now from its early years?

From the start, the mainstream of young adult literature has been perceived as realism. (However, to belabor the metaphor to a ridiculous degree, the genre can also be seen as two parallel streams—realism and fantasy. More about this later.) Although the prototype for style and voice was J. D. Salinger's *The Catcher in the Rye*, it was not until sixteen years later that that book's promise began to be fulfilled. In the magic years of 1967–1968, S. E. Hinton's *The Outsiders*, Robert Lipsyte's *The Contender*, and Paul Zindel's *The Pigman* broke away from the saccharine formula of the junior novel to confront bold new subjects that soon earned such novels the name of "the new realism." Other new writers like Richard Peck, Norma Klein, M. E. Kerr, and Norma and Harry Mazer took

Originally published in *Young Adult Literature in the 21st Century* by Pam B. Cole (Boston: McGraw-Hill Higher Education, 2009), pp. 66–68.

up the challenge of writing novels about serious adolescent realities without succumbing to didacticism.

Then in 1974 the publication of Robert Cormier's first YA novel, *The Chocolate War*, initiated a new level of literary excellence in the fledgling genre and also unleashed a storm of controversy about the darkness and hard truth-saying of his work, a type of controversy that became characteristic of the field in general in the following years. For the first time, a YA novel had confronted the broader human condition beyond the problems of adolescence. Cormier had disturbed the universe of young adult literature with his dark vision and complex ambiguities, and the stunned critical reception of the book led to the realization that fiction for teens could be great literature. With the publication of *I Am the Cheese* in 1977 and *After the First Death* in 1979, it became apparent that *The Chocolate War* had been not a single anomaly, but the beginning of a body of work, and other writers were freed to follow their own vision, wherever it led. Cormier continued to up the ante throughout the twenty-six years and fourteen novels of his career, and other writers rose to the challenge of honesty and excellence in their own ways.

However, changing trends in YA lit always come and usually go, both in the center and around the edges. In the early seventies a form arose that took books for teens in a less excellent direction. Emboldened by the new possibilities for writing about formerly taboo subjects, less skilled writers began to shape novels around social concerns, the more trendy the better. The "problem novel," as this variant came to be called, focused on the latest headlines for books about drugs, suicide, sexual molestation, prostitution, parents missing due to death or divorce or desertion, runaways, anorexia. "The subject matter too often became the tail that wagged the dog of the novel," says Michael Cart in his history of the genre, *From Romance to Realism*. The problem (or multiple problems), became the center, with all its statistics and possible outcomes, rather than a character or the writer's personal vision, and writers drew heavily on the possibilities for preachy moral instruction. These books were enormously popular with teens, but they grew sillier and sillier, until they were finally kidded to death by critics. The death knell was Daniel Pinkwater's delightful parody, *Young Adult Novel*. The influence of the problem novel is often exaggerated. It lasted only a decade and was a mere digression, as the main body of the literature continued to grow in scope, relevance, and sophistication.

However, one type of the problem novel preceded its heyday and continues with us to the present time. Stories of teenage pregnancy and parenting, affectionately called "preggers novels," began in 1966 with *A Girl Like Me* by Jeannette Eyerly. Other early such books were *My Darling, My Hamburger* by Paul Zindel (1969) and *Mr. and Mrs. BoJo Jones* by Ann Head (1971). The pattern followed a formula: worry, discovery, revelation to boyfriend and parents, choice of three alternatives—abortion, keeping the baby, and adoption—with authorial approval of the last option. This pattern gradually loosened and was addressed with more literary skill in the nineties, to grow beyond its problem-novel origins. Sometimes the point of view is even that of the young father, as in Angela Johnson's award-winning verse novel, *The First Part Last*.

But what about that second river of YA fiction, fantasy? Today it seems as if it has become the predominant form in the genre, at least for this decade. However, fantasy (and science fiction) has always drawn enthusiastic young readers. Tolkien's trilogy *The Lord of the Rings*, of course, was the beginning, with the American edition published in 1966. However, it took several years until that mighty work trickled down to teen awareness from its first readership on the college level. Then it was an overwhelming phenomenon, bringing young people to the joy of reading as Harry Potter would thirty years later. Another seminal work that began publication in 1968 was Ursula Le Guin's Earthsea trilogy. In the next decade, a few writers like H. M. Hoover wrote science fiction aimed at YA readers, most notably William Sleator with his behaviorist novel, *House of Stairs*. But not until the publication of *The Sword of Shannara* by Terry Brooks in 1977 did American writers take up the more-or-less medieval world in three volumes, the model set by Tolkien. The number of YA books based on this pattern, with its variant of the Arthurian novel, has grown steadily ever since, until legions of huge fantasy trilogies and series have come to dominate the YA market since 1993.

YA realism, meanwhile, has been enriched by a number of separate subject emphases that can, each in its own right, almost be thought of as subgenres. Most relevant to teens is sexuality, a subject that has been a major part of YA fiction since its beginning, and has often garnered the wrath of censors. The iconic book of sexual discovery is Judy Blume's *Forever*, appearing in 1975, just one year after *The Chocolate War* broke open the field to new challenges. Its frank celebration of human coupling has earned it a very long life and many readers. Although it is often said that *Forever* was unique in the reality of its portrayal of sexual activity, the truth is that during the sexual revolution of the seventies, there were many YA novels by Norma Klein and others that equaled its daring, if not its quality. Later, as AIDS made sexual intercourse a life-threatening practice, writers became leery of scenes of lovemaking. The sexual novel morphed into the AIDS novel, with M. E. Kerr's *Night Kites* (1986) and other books that showed us young people trying to make sense of the age of AIDS. Only recently, as the disease fades from the forefront of public consciousness, have YA authors begun to explore sexuality again in gritty novels like *Doing It* by Melvin Burgess (2004).

A related form is the novel of gay and lesbian awareness and identity. In his groundbreaking study of this literary type, *The Heart Has Its Reasons* (2006), Michael Cart traces the changes in the form. This theme has been a constant in YA fiction since John Donovan's *I'll Get There, It Better Be Worth the Trip* appeared in 1969. However, in the seventies the plot led inexorably to the death by automobile (or "death by gayness," as it jokingly came to be called) of the lead character or dog, presumably as a punishment. This trend came to be a running gag, and the form eventually grew beyond such naïveté. The first YA novel to deal with lesbian identity was *Ruby* by Rosa Guy (1976), but the icon has become *Annie on*

My Mind by Nancy Garden (1982). In later years, gay and lesbian characters have become a natural part of many YA novels without being seen as "the problem," and in 2003 David Levithan's *Boy Meets Boy* showed us a beautiful world where nobody is upset that the homecoming queen is also the star quarterback.

For a long while YA fiction depicted an all-white, mostly middle-class world. When multicultural awareness began to develop, the requirement was seen at first as a matter of making the history and presence of African Americans visible. A very early landmark book in this development was *I Know Why the Caged Bird Sings* by Maya Angelou (1969). In the seventies publishers actively encouraged black writers, and new voices emerged like Alice Childress, Rosa Guy, Virginia Hamilton, Mildred Taylor, and the great Walter Dean Myers, whose first YA novel was *Fast Sam, Cool Clyde, and Stuff* (1975). As with gay characters, in later years African American characters have come to be seen as people with lives and issues beyond their racial identity. With the surge of immigration from Asia and Central America in the nineties, a need for books exploring those realities has arisen. YA novels reflecting the lives of contemporary Asian American teens have been especially scarce, despite the many Chinese historical or mythological novels of Laurence Yep. The recent Printz winner *American Born Chinese* by Gene Luen Yang is a step in this direction, but there is still a long way to go. Hispanic YA fiction of all kinds, however, is growing well, adding to the longtime examples of Gary Soto, Sandra Cisneros, and several others. YA fiction showing the lives of contemporary Muslim teens is still to come, regrettably. As the tide of immigration continues, more books focus on the problems of immigrants as outsiders, and the complex self-definition of teens who have more than one ethnic or racial identity.

For many years historical novels were said to be anathema to teens, and very few were written or published. Not until the unprecedented success of the American Girls series did publishers begin to change their minds. Ann Rinaldi and Kathryn Lasky have been the workhorses in this subgenre, turning out novel after novel

of historical fiction. In the twenty-first century the form has grown
to new heights of creativity and originality, culminating in the two
books of *The Astonishing Life of Octavian Nothing* by M. T. Anderson (2006).

Some current subjects in realistic YA fiction hark back to the
problem novel without succumbing to the single-mindedness of
that form. However, the repetition of these themes is beginning
to become tiresome. Novels built around incidents of physical or
sexual abuse have been around for two decades, and there have
been some excellent books, like Cynthia Voigt's *When She Hol-
lers* (1994), Norma Fox Mazer's *When She Was Good* (1997), and
Laurie Halse Andersen's *Speak* (1999). After the shootings at Columbine High School there were a number of books about a shooter
who plans to bring a gun to school, but this theme, while important,
is beginning to feel overdone. And surely it is time to give plots a
rest that turn on alienation and overcoming bullies, either male or
female.

Forms other than the novel have also become part of young
adult fiction. The short story anthology, now a staple, began with
the first collection by the now well-known anthologist Don Gallo,
Sixteen (1984). The pattern, as set by Gallo, is to amass a group
of original stories by familiar YA authors centering on a theme.
These themes can range from quite specific, such as Gallo's recent
What Are You Afraid Of: Stories about Phobias (2006), to quite
amorphous, such as *All Sleek and Skimming* (2006), edited by Lisa
Heggum. Sex, gay and lesbian identity, and the supernatural have
been popular themes. Sometimes these collections can be by one
author, like Margo Lanagan's remarkable *Black Juice* (2005). An
interesting experiment growing from this form was Michael Cart's
Rush Hour, a quarterly literary journal encompassing not only short
stories but poetry and art. Teachers are fond of these collections for
their ability to snare short-attention-span readers and to fit neatly
in a day's teaching plan.

The verse novel is a form peculiar to young adult literature,
although narrative in verse is a very much older pattern, going

back to the earliest literature. The young adult verse novel was inadvertently invented by Mel Glenn, in his collection titled *Class Dismissed! High School Poems* (1982). Characteristically the verse novel is a novel-length story told in a series of free verse poems written in first person. In the best of these books each separate poem is its own little jewel. Sometimes there is a single narrator, but there can also be multiple voices. The verse sometimes has a formal rhyme scheme and sometimes just reflects the rhythms of natural speech, arranged in breath groups. There was a blossoming of this form in the late nineties and the first five years of the current century, but now they seem to have receded somewhat. A number of excellent books have been shaped as verse novels, the very best being *Out of the Dust* by Karen Hesse (1997), *Make Lemonade* (1993) by Virginia Euwer Wolff, and its National Book Award–winning sequel, *True Believer* (2001).

Graphic novels were popular in Europe for many years before they were accepted in America, and I wrote about the appeal of this form in my "YA Perplex" column for *Wilson Library Bulletin* in the early eighties. But not until the last five years has this comics-inspired genre been enthusiastically embraced by teens and librarians. Now there are many guidebooks and websites to educate teachers and librarians who are latecomers to the form, and several mainstream YA publishers have moved into the field with graphic novel imprints, such as Roaring Brooks' First Second. Art Spiegelman's great Holocaust memoir *Maus* won the Pulitzer Prize in 1992, and much later, when Gene Luen Yang was given the Printz Award for *American Born Chinese* in 2006, the graphic novel finally came to be respected as a valid literary form in America.

Audiobooks and other electronic forms look to the future, although they will probably continue to be supplements, rather than replacements for the print book. Many YA books are now published simultaneously as print and audiobooks, and the popularity of the electronic version with teens is high, especially with those who do not read well or who are new English learners.

Up to now, we have been looking only at hardcover YA fiction, but some of the most volatile YA publishing trends have been acted out in paperbacks. The tendency of librarians, teachers, and critics to deplore this popular sub-literature is a very old one, going back to the example of the Stratemeyer Syndicate, a writing factory that churned out the Nancy Drew and Hardy Boys series, among others, in the first half of the twentieth century. In the beginnings of young adult literature, paperbacks were limited to reprints of previously published hardcover books. But in 1971, with the astounding success of *Go Ask Alice* by Beatrice Sparks, it began to dawn on publishers that teens would buy their own books, if they were the *right* books. Previous purchasers of YA books had been teachers, parents, and librarians, but now, with this new market, more hardcover YA titles were translated into paperback.

With the advent of the indoor shopping mall as a teen hangout, the stage was set for a wider marketing plan. Gambling that teens were tired of the gritty reality of the problem novel, and perhaps frightened by AIDS, publishers in the eighties began to bring out sweet, clean, conventional paperback romance series, like Wildfire, Sweet Dreams, Young Love, First Love, Wishing Star, Caprice, and Sweet Valley High. They were an instant sensation with young girls, who bought them by the armload. The enormous significance of this move was that these were *original* paperbacks, not reprints. Librarians deplored; feminists wrung their hands. I wrote, "The books that are found in the chain bookstores are of far lower quality and aimed at much younger readers than those that are found on the similarly labeled shelves in public libraries. The whole field has become strangely bifurcated and we seem to be moving in the direction of two separate literatures."

The separatist trend continued as romance phased into horror paperbacks, beginning with Christopher Pike's *Slumber Party* in 1985, and continued on into the nineties. As the teen population declined to a new low in numbers, publishers desperate to keep this new market turned to ever more sensational and trashy paperbacks, finally descending into the abyss with R. L. Stine's execrable

Goosebumps and Fear Street series. At library conferences publishers and librarians moaned to each other that YA was dead.

Not hardly. Today, as we have said, the roaring mainstream of young adult literature is overflowing its banks. There is an all-time high of more than thirty million teens in the United States, and that growth is not expected to peak until 2010. Teens account for a major part of bookstore sales, and they're not buying just popular paperbacks. Trends continue, yes, like the currently ubiquitous chick lit, but the best of YA lit now appears right alongside it on bookstore shelves. There are more literary and challenging books for older teens being written, often with strikingly original stylistic innovations and sophisticated themes. More formerly adult writers are moving into this fertile field of young adult literature, like Joyce Carol Oates, Alice Hoffman, James Patterson, and Carl Hiassen, while the writers of the YA canon like Chris Lynch and M. T. Anderson get better with every book. The Printz Award, the National Book Award, and the *Los Angeles Times* Book Prize have recognized the quality of young adult literature, and the day is not far off when YA masterworks will be seen not as "kids' books," but simply as great works of human literature.

Twayne and Scarecrow

An Editor's Memoir

ONCE UPON A TIME—SAY, 1983—there was almost no serious literature about young adult literature—except, of course, the basic standard work, *Literature for Today's Young Adults* by Ken Donelson and Alleen Pace Nilsen. I had been trying since 1978 to create a body of critical work in my "YA Perplex" column for the *Wilson Library Bulletin*, and other critics like Michael Cart, Betsy Hearne, and Zena Sutherland had done some thoughtful reviews and essays, but all that lacked the dignity of pages between two hard covers. And then I heard that somebody was planning a series of biocritical studies on young adult authors, and the editor was to be a young adult specialist at Boston Public Library, Ron Brown. And I had his phone number.

I stubbed my toe rushing to call him. "Dibs!" I cried. "Dibs on Robert Cormier!" Ron gave me a thumbs-up, and so it began. The "somebody" who was doing the series turned out to be Twayne Publishers, a division of G. K. Hall and a venerable and dignified outfit that had a long history of turning out respectable literary criticism. But could they tolerate the more lively tone I envisioned for a study of a body of work read by teens? All my fears were put to rest when I met my in-house editor Athenaide Dallett. The daughter of concert duo pianists, she was young, witty, creative, very bright, and

Originally published in *The ALAN Review* 36, no. 2 (winter 2009): 64–70.

eager to learn about young adult fiction. She had already found her beginning point in the works of Robert Cormier and was reading her way through his novels with amazed pleasure.

And "amazed pleasure" was my reaction, too, when the Cormiers graciously invited me to visit them at their home in Leominster, Massachusetts. There I interviewed Bob nonstop for two days, except for the time we spent having an afternoon beer or two and the hours I happily delved into the riches of the Cormier Archive at the Fitchburg College library. I went home and immersed myself in the subtle complexities and puzzles of his novels, and in 1985 the debut of Twayne's Young Adult Author series was celebrated with the publication of the first volume, *Presenting Robert Cormier*. The occasion was observed with speeches and a gala presentation at the Boston Public Library Authors series and a reception and signing (by both Bob and I) at the Boston Bookstore Café. My delight in the display window full of what Bob always called "our book" and my pleasure at speaking to an audience of distinguished Boston literati was undimmed by the fact that I had come down with the flu and had a fever of 103° as I stepped up to the podium.

Meanwhile, series editor Ron Brown had been lining up other people to write about the leading YA authors. In 1985, choosing the subjects was simple—YA lit had a canon of about twenty-five "big names," and that was it. Ron recruited writers from among his friends and Boston colleagues to tackle his choice of the first six biggies and, encouraged by the critics' grateful applause, settled down to nurture and edit the growing series. The second book to be published was *Presenting M. E. Kerr* by Alleen Pace Nilsen, who was already not only the coauthor of the aforesaid *Literature for Today's Young Adults,* but also a past president of the Assembly on Literature for Adolescents (ALAN), a selection pattern that was to be repeated many times in the series. And then in 1986 Ron had a Thoreau-like epiphany about the shape of his life and moved on to live in the country, while I inherited the editorship of the nascent series.

Athenaide Dallett and I took over the editing of the works in progress. In the beginning we exchanged long editorial letters before we passed our thoughts on to the writers, and from her brilliance as an editor I learned how to spot the places where changes would improve a manuscript—and how to communicate those changes to a writer tactfully, with encouragement instead of criticism. Athenaide became my mentor, my staunch ally in sticky editorial situations, and to this day a valued and admired friend.

Acquisition was now in my lap, so I went straight to the top, to the godfather of ALAN, Don Gallo. I offered him the biggest fish in my pond—Richard Peck—and he couldn't refuse. But there was a problem. Richard didn't want to be biographized. With becoming modesty, he demurred, explaining that he felt his writing wasn't worthy of a whole book of analysis—an assessment, even at that point in his career, that was obviously dead wrong. Nevertheless, Don and I persisted. I wrote cajoling notes and letters (to this day one does not communicate with Richard Peck by e-mail), and finally he agreed to be the subject of a Twayne study. Don wrote it, but in four years Richard had several more major novels, and it was necessary to update the study, and now, in 2008, Don Gallo and coauthor Wendy Glenn are about to publish the definitive work on Peck, including all the rich writing of his maturity, for Twayne's successor series, the Scarecrow Studies in Young Adult Literature.

As I added more authors, I laid down some guidelines for the series' detailed content and style. Our target audience was three-fold—YA librarians, teachers, and students—and so we wanted the books to be lively and readable but to offer sound critical insights and talking points for class discussion. I also wanted the subject author to come alive as a person in these pages, and so I encouraged my writers to do personal interviews and even get themselves invited to the author's home. "Find out the dog's name," I told them. "Notice the state of the writing desk. And don't back away from the hard questions."

From my own experience doing hundreds of interviews for an earlier book, *Passing the Hat*, I wrote detailed instructions for interviewing ("unwrap your tapes before you get there. . . ."). The series guidelines also dealt with other stylistic and practical matters, such as when to refer to the subject author by first name (only in the preface) and when to use terms like "children" or "youngsters" for YAs (never). A persistent difficulty in the early days was writers' tendencies to confuse the instruction to "write lively" with permission to use slang and inappropriate colloquial expressions. Nowadays, that tendency has faded away and has been replaced with a different fault—stilted academic jargon and feminist rhetoric.

A stylistic problem with legal implications was Twayne's policy of a 400-word limit on quoted material, even from the works of the subject author. Although I stressed this matter in the guidelines, nearly every writer exceeded the limit. I spent many tedious hours counting words and adding up the totals—and then shaking my finger at the writer. Holding quotes down was especially difficult for those working with highly quotable authors—like Richard Peck. The better the author, the more difficult it is to avoid picking up that author's apt phrases and colorful descriptions, and to this day, the problem persists with the series. But I hasten to assure writers who grieve at the need to cut that the book will be better with their own carefully considered words.

One matter that I couldn't change was the title format. Some people had even begun to refer to it as the "Presenting Series," so name recognition won out over style and grace. But another feature of the first two books that both Athenaide and I joined forces to alter was the clumsy drawings used as illustrations. These were universally deplored by our writers and the critics, so with the third volume, *Presenting Norma Fox Mazer*, we switched to photos supplied by the subject author.

As the series grew, I found that I had to change my preconception that the writers could be drawn from my American Library Association network of YA librarians. I found that working librarians do not have spare time to write nor do working teachers, with a very few exceptions. However, it dawned on me that academics are *expected* to write, and their bosses smile on the time and effort that takes. And as I became more involved with ALAN, I realized that here was a concentrated collection of passionate and articulate supporters of young adult literature who were eager to produce books for Twayne. As I drew on this pool of writers, the series became almost a who's who of excellence in ALAN leadership. Of the thirty-five ALAN presidents since 1983, fifteen have written books for the series, and of the fifty-nine titles in the combined Twayne and Scarecrow series, thirty were written by ALAN leadership, including both executive secretaries. Old ALAN hands will recognize many familiar names in the bibliographies that accompany this piece.

One of the great pleasures in editing the Twayne series was matching subject authors with congenial writers. Joanne Brown and Kathryn Lasky, two witty Jewish mothers, hit it off beautifully, as did passionate shoppers Paula Danziger and Kathleen Krull. Ted Hipple charmed me into giving him a contract to write about his fellow Tennessee author, Sue Ellen Bridgers. But perhaps my best match was Terry Davis with his college friend Chris Crutcher. Terry, as a fine YA author himself, wrote a brilliant biographical chapter in the shape of a long fictional motorcycle journey, which I very reluctantly axed because it didn't fit the rest of the book, but his intimate knowledge of the dynamics of Crutcher's family provided invaluable insights into the author's work. Other joys were the unexpected discoveries that emerged about authors we thought we knew: William Sleator's years as a ballet pianist; Barbara Wersba's early career as an actress (with a glamour photo to prove it on the cover); the Mazers as radical political activists in their youth.

An inherent problem in trying to analyze authors in the middle of their careers is how to fit future works by that author into a current evaluation. I ran into that difficulty very early with the first edition of *Presenting Robert Cormier,* when I tried to gather together and interpret all his themes with what I thought was a very neat metaphor about an implacable force. But Bob read it, of course, and it made him so self-conscious that none of his later novels fit my tidy interpretation. Criticism can influence creation, for good or bad. Trying to catch up with a prolific author, too, can be a breathless race, as Gary Salvner discovered in writing about Gary Paulsen.

I began to tell writers to ask to see unpublished books in production or even books in progress.

As the series went on, I started to feel that it was getting too formulaic, and so I looked for new ideas to add to the successful basic format. Science fiction and the newly emerging genre of fantasy troubled me because to cover these genres adequately, it would be necessary to look at many minor authors, as well as a constellation of big names. But it was a type of writing that I had publicly deplored despite its popularity that became the subject of the first Twayne series genre study with *Presenting Young Adult Horror Fiction* by the irrepressible Cosette Kies. Science fiction and fantasy had to wait, the first until I found a writer fresh enough to the genre to be objective in Suzanne Reid, and the second for eight years, while *VOYA* editor Cathi MacRae desperately tried to organize, read, and make sense of the rapidly expanding field of fantasy. (Characteristically, Cathi insisted on including short book reviews by teens over my initial objections but later approval.)

During these years there were changes at Twayne Publishers. In 1989 Athenaide was promoted out of my reach and later left to get a master's degree at Georgetown University, and Liz Traynor Fowler took her job as in-house series editor. Later the position was passed to Jennifer Farthing. Between 1985 and 1989, six of the early titles were updated for a Dell paperback reprint series titled Laurel-Leaf Library of Young Adult Authors. By 1995, Macmillan had replaced G. K. Hall. And then in 1997 market pressures forced Twayne to stop acquiring new titles, and two years later Macmillan Library Reference was sold to the Gale Group and the series was cancelled, despite good reviews and excellent sales. (For a list of Twayne's Young Adult Author Series, see the appendix.)

But I was having too much fun editing "my" series to give it up, and besides, I had made promises to writers who were at work on as-yet-unpublished books for the now defunct series. So I looked around and settled on Scarecrow Press, primarily because that was where Dorothy Broderick and Mary K. Chelton had taken their essential YA magazine, *Voice of Youth Advocates*. Also, I had worked with editorial director Shirley Lambert and anticipated that she and I would see eye to eye about the series' future. We did, and we hammered out a title: "Scarecrow Studies in Young Adult Literature" (although I lobbied for "Young Adult Authors and Issues"). In this new situation I made lots of room for fresh ideas, keeping the successful single author and genre formats, but also opening up a broader perspective to include issue studies and anything else that might come under the heading "YA lit crit."

The first volume stretched my commitment to innovation. R. L. Stine was a controversial phenomenon at the time for his wildly popular Goosebumps and Fear Street paperbacks, and the brilliant and unpredictable Patrick Jones wanted to use Stine as a jumping-off place to examine the value of literary popular culture. This struck me as a great book idea, even though I personally abhor trashy popular horror fiction. So I wrote Patrick, "I will take care not to step on your opinions, as long as you justify them." And then I added, "I think we're going to have some fun with this." And we did, as we argued back and forth in the margins of the developing manuscript. In 1998 *What's So Scary about R. L. Stine?* was published as the first volume in the new series, sporting a new look with a laminated cover design and, instead of internal family snapshots as illustrations, a truly scary photo of Stine, warts and all, as a frontispiece.

During the writing of the book, Patrick and I scoured our networks to find a way to get an interview with Stine, but the walls protecting him held firm. With the help of an editor friend I even had a carefully composed letter carried into the fortress and hand-delivered to Stine's wife, but there was no response. Then, weeks after the book was published, Patrick got an e-mail from Stine, thanking him and praising the book lavishly. "I had no idea such a work was in the works," he wrote. "Why didn't you and I ever get to talk?" We gnashed our teeth.

Chris Crowe had had better luck in getting to the notoriously reclusive Mildred Taylor, but his fine study of that author stayed behind at Twayne and became the last book in that series. The

Scarecrow series began to grow and gain good reviews, in spite of a bumpy time with the second book. As the completed manuscript of Jeanne McGlinn's *Ann Rinaldi: Historian and Storyteller* went into production, a huge controversy exploded over Rinaldi's depiction of government Indian schools in her novel *My Heart Is on the Ground.* "Hold the presses," I shouted. McGlinn, at my request, rewrote her analysis of that book and added an acknowledgement of the issues raised by Native American advocates, especially Deborah Reese, who had written a scathing review, and Beverly Slapin, editor of the website Oyate. But some good came out of this brouhaha, as out of it emerged the right person to do an entire book on the now obviously sensitive issue of Native Americans in YA lit—Paulette Molin.

As the series developed, I continued to select leading authors as subjects of studies. Arthea Reed was a logical choice to write about Norma Fox Mazer, since she knew the couple's history through her Twayne book on Harry Mazer. Edith Tyson gladly took on Orson Scott Card instead of the book on YA Christian fiction in which she had become bogged down. I made sure David Gill understood surfing and Hawaiian culture before assigning him to write about Graham Salisbury. Ten other authors were captured for the series, but still there were some who eluded me, either because they felt the time was not right for them, or because I continued to search for exactly the right writer.

Studies of broad YA literary issues became a strong component of the series—empowered girls, sports, humor, guys, historical fiction, and a delightful discussion of names in young adult novels, a subject Alleen Pace Nilsen had wanted to write about since her Twayne book on M. E. Kerr. Recent titles tackle the growing YA theme of mixed heritage, explore the history of girls' series books, take a hard look at body image and female sexuality, and discuss serious issues of the depiction of animals in YA lit.

An obvious subject need was a book on gay, lesbian, bisexual, and transgendered characters and themes, and the obvious person to write it was the great Michael Cart. For years he was interested but too busy. I waited. Finally, in 2006, he and coauthor Christine Jenkins produced the definitive book on gay and lesbian issues in YA lit—*The Heart Has Its Reasons*—and it quickly became our best-seller. And one book that defied classification was *Lost Masterworks of Young Adult Literature*. Its editor, the magnificently organized Connie Zitlow, was inundated with offers from well-known YA writers and critics to sound off in essays about their own favorite forgotten titles.

Talking with renowned editor Marc Aronson one day, I had an epiphany. "How would you feel about doing a collection of your essays and speeches?" I asked. He felt fine about it, and the two books in which he gathered his audacious and literate writings became steady sellers for Scarecrow. Emboldened by this success, I asked Michael Cart for a collection of *his* articles and essays, and although his "Cart Blanche" columns were already spoken for by *Booklist*, he put together a thoughtful and enjoyable compilation, *Passions and Pleasures*.

Perhaps the most fun I had with editing the series came with Walter Hogan's delicious book about the quirky comic genius, Daniel Pinkwater. As chapters arrived in the mail, I couldn't resist tearing open the manila envelope on the way home from the mail-box to delight in the latest installment of Hogan's droll discussion of Pinkwater's equally droll novels, with voluminous and amusing footnotes. Walter was in close touch with Pinkwater all along, so when it came time to choose a catchy title, it was Pinkie's sugges-tion of *The Agony and the Eggplant* that caught my fancy with its sheer absurdity. But would my editor Shirley buy it? I ran it past her, and there was a long thoughtful silence. Then she smiled. "I love it!" she cried. However, Pinkwater's choice of a cover—himself with five rhinoceroses—was just too far out, and so we settled for a photo in which the large author is painting a picture on his own palm.

YA literary criticism has come a long way since 1983. Several publishers are now doing excellent author studies of one shape or an-other, and there have been many useful annotated bibliographies of various subjects. It can be said in all honesty that there is now lots of serious literature about young adult literature. And lots more to come as the genre grows beyond our wildest predictions. As I look over my list of works in progress for Scarecrow Studies in Young Adult Literature, I think I can promise that we will continue to pounce on the best new authors, tear open the most challenging issues, and spring a surprise or two. (For a list of the books in the Scarecrow Studies in Young Adult Literature series, see the series pages in the front of this book.)

Part Two

TRENDS AND TENDENCIES

Drowning in Success

"And thick and fast they came at last, / and more, and more, and more—" as Tweedledee said to Alice about supplicant oysters. This year his words apply just as well to young adult publishing. My office shelves, usually more than adequate to hold a year's worth of YA fiction, overflow with enticing and provocative novels—fat fantasies, sequels to sequels, first volumes of new trilogies, books by famous authors, and those by first-time novelists. There are books ranged on the desk, the couch, the floor. What accounts for this sudden leap? What does it mean, and will it last?

Last June, *Wall Street Journal* called YA "one of the book industry's healthiest segments" and quoted estimates by Albert Greco, an industry analyst at Fordham University, that YA sales at that time were up 23 percent since 1999. In comparison, the *Journal* reported that adult sales in the same period were down slightly more than 1 percent. "YA is where it's at," says Karen Wojtyla, executive editor at Margaret K. McElderry Books, who sees "a general feeling of excitement over young adult literature" among publishers.

Demographics, of course, is the first explanation that leaps to mind. Children of baby boomers began to reach adolescence several years ago, and *60 Minutes* reported in September that between

Originally published in "The Sand in the Oyster," *Horn Book* (January/February 2006): 61–65.

1982 and 1995 eighty million of them were born, making these so-called echo boomers the largest generation of young people since the 1960s. Most important for the book publishing industry, these kids have an estimated $170 billion a year to spend. But do they spend it on books? Joe Monti, children's book buyer for Barnes & Noble, confirms that they most certainly do. In contrast to the accepted wisdom that librarians and teachers are the market for hardcover young adult books, he sees evidence that although book purchases may be filtered through the wallets of parents and librarians, word-of-mouth among teens is the motivating factor for sales. "Readership is driving it," he says.

The Harry Potter phenomenon is the next most obvious explanation, in its almost mystically vast accomplishment of convincing huge numbers of teens—and adults—that reading children's books is fun. Certainly its effect is undeniable and clearly observable not only to bookstores and libraries but to anyone who relates to young people. The corollary is the enormous growth of fantasy and the development of a class of voracious fantasy readers, to the point where at least some elements of the fantastical appear in about half of current young adult novels. And it should be noted that as Harry grows older, so do his readers, and hence the literary sophistication and darkness of his later adventures. Thus preteens who began with Harry eight years ago are finding his recent story still relevant to their lives. Another consequence, according to Wojtyla, is that Harry Potter showed publishers that adults would read a book with a young teen protagonist, thus opening the door for novels like *The Life of Pi* by Yann Martel and *The Curious Incident of the Dog in the Night-Time* by Mark Haddon. However, Pottermania is not the whole explanation for the rise of YA publishing. As Ginee Seo, editor of her own imprint at Atheneum, notes, referring to best-selling realistic novelist Laurie Halse Anderson, "The *Harry Potter* reader is not the *Speak* reader."

In addition, Monti points out an influencing factor that is *not* so obvious but highly relevant for YA public librarians. About six years ago Barnes & Noble (and many other chain bookstores, I would suspect) moved their young adult sections away from the children's area and began treating YA as a special-reader genre like mystery or science fiction rather than an age-segregated literature. The result was a whopping double-digit increase in sales. Perhaps the proximity of young adult books to the adult shelves gives YA a new grown-up respectability in teens' eyes. The move also facilitates the display of crossover titles such as Christopher Paolini's *Eragon* and *Eldest* or Libba Bray's *A Great and Terrible Beauty* and *Rebel Angels*. Monti admits to a small but growing adult readership for YA fiction, maybe because of the same browsing accessibility.

What about the benefits of the Michael Printz Award for best young adult novel, hopefully dubbed the "YA Newbery"? Or the young reader category in the National Book Award or the *Los Angeles Times* Book Prize? How influential have these honors been in bringing young adult literature respect and attention from the larger literary world? Editors Seo and Wojtyla both credit them with giving greater visibility to the genre. "A spotlight has been put on a literature which had not previously gotten much attention," Wojtyla says. Several other editors have observed that the recognition of literary excellence by the Printz has given publishers incentive to seek out more high-quality young adult novels. Wojtyla also sees as another result a proliferation of MFA programs for writing for children and teens and a plethora of young graduates from these programs who often head directly to the YA genre.

On the other hand, bookseller Monti feels these awards have minimal effect. The National Book Award young reader prize he singles out in particular as being underreported in the media, although he admits that the Printz has an effect on the sales of single titles. Teen buzz, however, is far more important, he maintains. Although literary awards are important to librarians and parents, well-targeted activities by bookstores and large libraries may perhaps be as influential in bringing a particular YA novel to readers' attention. For example, every three months the booksellers of Barnes & Noble select a book by a first-time novelist to be featured in their Discover plan and given a "day in the sun" with conspicuous displays and promotion for twelve weeks. Lately these titles have often been YA novels such as David Levithan's *Boy Meets Boy*, John Green's *Looking for Alaska*, and Laura Whitcomb's *A Certain Slant of Light*.

A final contribution to the new dignity of YA lit, and one that has been mentioned with loutish amazement by the uninformed general press, is the invasion of young adult literature by well-known authors of books for adults. Alice Hoffman, Joyce Carol Oates, Carl Hiaasen, and Isabel Allende, among others, have tried their hands at the YA novel with varying success, and now these four were back last year for another round, with the addition of mystery writer Peter Abrahams and several more. Why would these literary stars "stoop" to a genre that has been seen in the past as "kiddie lit"? Maybe it's because of the stylistic freedom possible in young adult literature or, on the other hand, the interesting challenge of writing within the rather strict structural demands of the YA novel. Perhaps it may simply be, unlikely as it would have seemed in the past, that YA fiction can sometimes be more lucrative than adult. Monti, with his access to Barnes & Noble's sales figures, opines that the YA novel *Hoot* has been adult writer Carl Hiaasen's most profitable book. *Wall Street Journal* mentions occasional six-figure advances for second YA novels, and for Christopher Paolini's *Eldest,* a one-million-copy print run in anticipation of the film version of *Eragon*.

What's the downside of this sudden flood of glory for YA lit? It can actually be a problem for book review sources, award committees, and book buyers. How is it possible to effectively evaluate so many titles with a mechanism designed for far fewer? Linda Benson, book review editor for *Voice of Youth Advocates*, finds herself hard-pressed this year to live up to that magazine's goal of reviewing everything published in English for teens. She expects to see three thousand titles (admittedly much of it series nonfiction) before the year is out, and she has only enough space to review about one thousand. And how are budget-challenged YA librarians to make selections from such an embarrassment of riches? Personally, looking at all the books in my office that I know the award committees and I will never be able to get around to reading, I worry about the unacknowledged masterpieces hidden there that may vanish without a trace. Because the YA genre, like teens themselves, focuses on the new, the current, the latest hot thing, and most of last year's books, with only a few exceptions, are forgotten.

But returning to our cause for rejoicing, we still have to ask what will happen when the demographic wave passes and the seventh Harry Potter is finally backlisted. Will the number of books stay high; will this new visibility and respect for young adult literature last? Monti, with his focus on the reader, thinks it will. "Kids growing up with young adult literature now are going to stay with it through high school," he predicts, because there are now so many excellent YA novels for older teens. As he watched the wave pass through the middle-grade years from his vantage point as children's book buyer, he saw a rise and then a slowing down, but not a dip to the previous level. Yet Wojtyla quotes the old adage, "The only rule in publishing is that it's going to change."

YA Lit and the Deathly Fellows

THE DEAD WALK THE PAGES of recent young adult novels. These deathly fellows stroll through the literature in great numbers, contemplating their own demise and advising and annoying the living. In the last two years, by my admittedly casual count, there have been more than twenty-five novels and short stories in which the narrator is dead or in the process of dying, other dead characters have speaking parts, or Death himself has a role. And then there are always murder mysteries, traditional ghost stories, thrillers and war novels, and vampire tales.

However, the broader contemplation of mortality has spread throughout young adult literature in a multitude of books in which the end of life is a presence or motivating force. This trend began with Alice Sebold's highly successful 2002 adult novel, *The Lovely Bones*, which was widely read by young adults. Its then-fresh premise—a newly murdered teen speaks from heaven—led so many YA authors to frame novels around deathly monologues and conversations with the deceased that to list them all would turn this column into an annotated bibliography. Preeminent among them is *The Book Thief* by Marcus Zusak, narrated by the wry voice of Death itself. But many other authors introduced dead characters. Chris Crutcher dropped a talkative dead best friend into the plot of *The*

Originally published in "Borderlands," *Horn Book* (May/June 2008): 357–61.

Sledding Hill, as did Pete Hautman in *Invisible*. First-time novelist
Laura Whitcomb dealt ravishingly with the fleshly difficulties of two
dead lovers in *A Certain Slant of Light*. Gary Soto killed his protagonist in a men's room in the first chapter of *The Afterlife*. Deborah
Noyes edited *The Restless Dead*, a stunning necrobibliographic collection of stories by some of YA's best, including "The Gray Boy's
Work," by M. T. Anderson, in which a dead drummer boy follows a
deserter home and becomes a member of the family—and a symbol
of the ex-soldier's disgrace. In the same collection Kelly Link's young
poet has a surprise when he digs up "The Wrong Grave" to retrieve
a sheaf of poems buried a year earlier in the arms of his girlfriend
and finds a long-haired stranger taunting him from the coffin. And
the 2008 Printz Award went to a deathly fellow, as Geraldine Mc-
Caughrean's teenage Sym slogged bravely through *The White Darkness* of Antarctica, teased and encouraged by her main crush, the
ninety-years-dead—and extremely charming—Captain Titus Oates
from Scott's South Pole expedition.

Witnessing the actual process of dying, however, is as close as
we get in this life to knowing about the experience of death, and although there have always been plenty of YA novels about a beloved
somebody dying (Lurlene McDaniel has built an entire literary
empire on the four-hankie grief-fest), these stories are nearly always
from the point of view of the survivor. It is in books where the *protagonist* is dying that we come closest to the reality of death. Several
recent YA novels feature terminally ill narrators. Sonya Hartnett's
Printz Honor book *Surrender* opens with an extraordinary chapter
that spares nothing in showing the small indignities and nastiness
of a worn-out body dying in slow torment from natural causes—
except that at the end of the passage we find with cold shock that
the decrepit expiring body that we are in bed with belongs not to
an old man but to a youth of twenty. Chris Crutcher's extraordinary
and courageous novel *Deadline* seems at first to follow the same
path in its story of an eighteen-year-old about to die but takes a
more encouraging route as the young man decides to keep the di-
agnosis of cancer secret and to live the last year of his life as fully

as possible. An inevitable comparison arises with Jenny Downham's rich and deeply moving *Before I Die*, in which a girl dying of leukemia accomplishes her endgame goal of falling in love.

Suicide has always been a staple of YA lit, at least the part about how family and friends feel afterward. But there has been a recent spate of stories examining suicidal thoughts and actions from the perpetrator's point of view. The most original in structure is *Thirteen Reasons Why* by Jay Asher, in which the dead girl becomes a technologically supported voice from the grave by mailing a set of tapes to thirteen of her peers, explaining in excruciating detail why each one of them is guilty of an action that led her to kill herself. Two innovative and daring suicide novels have examined the motivations and mind-set of a suicide bomber: *In the Name of God* by Paula Jolin, in which a devout young Muslim woman is seduced by the idea of sacrificing herself, and *The Innocent's Story* by Nicky Singer, which uses a dead narrator to get inside the troubled mind of the terrorist who has killed her.

When these dead fellows are not narrating or influencing the action in novels, where do they go? YA writers have imagined a wide variety of depictions of "heaven" but have almost never availed themselves of traditional Christian theology about the afterlife as a dimension outside of time where the soul returns to God. Some authors have been audacious enough to attempt to give us a literal picture of the afterworld, as in Margo Lanagan's horrifying evocation of purgatory in a story in her most recent collection, *Red Spikes*. In "Under Hell, Over Heaven," four teens have lost all emotion as they slog back and forth between paradise and hell delivering the damned and the redeemed to their respective final destinations. Other writers offer less literal versions, in which the afterworld resembles either a skycam for observing the action on Earth or a waiting room in eternity where wrongs are made right. Most chilling is Philip Pullman's concept, in *The Amber Spyglass*, of a place like ancient Hades, where crowds of sad shades are condemned to mill about like human cattle in an eternal twilight world. Most poetic, Sonya Hartnett invokes at least a whiff of the fragrance of the traditional idea of heaven in the last sentence of *Surrender*: "Wings unfold around me and, with a mighty sweep of air, I alone am lifted skyward, from where I first arrived." And most satisfying is Harry Potter's "death," spent in a place of reconciliation, the railroad station to Hogwarts called, significantly, King's Cross. Other depictions of the afterlife are ingenious in their variety: Gabrielle Zevin imagines an afterworld where everyone gets younger all the time (*Elsewhere*); John Ritter depicts a homey kitchen where a mysterious character named the InDoc cooks bacon and eggs and helps dead soldiers get in touch with their guilt for killing ("Baseball in Iraq" in *Dreams and Visions*, edited by M. Jerry Weiss and Helen Weiss). And *Heaven Looks a Lot Like the Mall* by Wendy Mass is self-explanatory.

A puzzling aspect of this trend is that nowhere do we find spiritual questioning on the part of the dying or any consolation of faith. The characters never turn to prayer for release from suffering, for peace, for comfort for their grieving relatives and friends. Church ladies are not there to send casseroles, the clergy are not called in to help the transition of the soul, and God is not blamed or invoked in any way—except by the suicide bombers who call on Allah. There is only a bleak sense of ending, of an imminent black nothingness. In *Before I Die* Tessa says about heaven, "I think it's a great big lie. When you're dead, you're dead."

So if spiritual exploration is not the point, what *is* behind all this interest in death on the part of YA authors? Has the subject surfaced so intensely as a reflection of our perilous times? Or is it because suburban teens are bored with their seemingly safe existence and want scary extremes? Teens, as the cliché goes, think they are immortal. Is it more comfortable for them than for adults to read close-up accounts of death, since they are theoretically further away from having to accept their own mortality?

These are all marginal explanations, but I think the more central answer is that this trend simply reflects writers' discovery of a new area, a new direction, a new twist on good old adolescent angst. YA critic Jonathan Hunt has posited that "the dead narrator gives the narrative a sense of immediacy that is so characteristic of young adult fiction, but at the same time allows for a degree of reflection and self-awareness that would probably otherwise seem jarring for a young adult narrator." And grown-ups who worry that this is a morbid tendency should be reassured that all this looking at death can only put trivial teen difficulties in perspective and make every minute of life seem even sweeter.

So What *Really* Happened?

As YOUNG ADULT LITERATURE GROWS stylistically fancier, the qualities of ambivalence and ambiguity, as well as the related consequence of the unresolved ending, appear more frequently. When do these qualities add to the effectiveness of a book, and when are they merely an annoyance? How do they fit the definition of story as a necessary chain of causality, with a beginning, a middle, and an end? And how do they relate to Eliza Dresang's assertion, in her groundbreaking study *Radical Change*, that one of the key markers of postmodern literature is interactivity between text and reader?

Ambivalence and ambiguity are similar in meaning but not synonymous. *Ambivalence* refers to the coexistence of conflicting feelings or thoughts toward an action, person, or idea, while *ambiguity* refers to something that is open to multiple interpretations. Although they are most commonly seen as inseparable in fiction, either can appear by itself, as evidenced by a number of Robert Cormier's novels. For example, *After the First Death* is drenched in ambiguity about the identity of narrators, their sanity or suicide, although our horror at the gunshot with which Miro accidentally kills Kate at the end is anything but ambivalent. But in both *Heroes* and *The Rag and Bone Shop*, the ending is indeterminate, with the protagonist leaving the scene with a weapon—a gun in *Heroes* and

Originally published in "The Sand in the Oyster," *Horn Book* (July/August 2005): 503–7.

a knife in *The Rag and Bone Shop*—that he may or may not use in a certain way. Leave it to Cormier to roll ambivalence and ambiguity together so compellingly. In *Tenderness* we finish the book with ambivalent feelings of compassion and revulsion for the serial killer Eric Poole, this time requiring from us not a choice of two options but a disturbing, simultaneous experience of both emotions.

As these examples suggest, Robert Cormier loved ambiguity and ambivalence and used them well. Indeed, he can be credited with introducing these provocative literary devices into young adult fiction—and paying a high price for that innovation. On its publication in 1974, *The Chocolate War* infuriated some critics with an ending that defied readers' expectations. Instead of fulfilling the American myth of the lone hero winning against the forces of evil, Cormier gave us an ending that raised a squirming handful of conflicting feelings and multiple interpretations. The novel has been the object of censorship attack ever since, and in 2004 it was, not for the first time, number one on the American Library Association's list of censors' targets. With the growing sophistication of young adult fiction in recent years, other YA writers—Walter Dean Myers, Lois Lowry, Terry Trueman, and David Almond, among others—have been able to use ambiguity and ambivalence almost without negative reaction.

But why are these literary devices so disturbing and at the same time so delightfully intriguing? Despite the digital age's growing acceptance of nonlinearity, when the pieces of a story are presented randomly or a piece is left out or is open to multiple interpretations, we have a strong impulse to organize those pieces in the "right" —or linear—order and to "fix" any unclear links in the chain of story. Dresang quotes Mark Turner's theory that the need to arrange events in a logical sequence—that is, to tell stories—seems to be inherent in the human brain. Ambiguity and ambivalence disturb that order and tug at us to be resolved; we need to turn the story over in our minds, talk to others about it, decide "what really happened." Or, as the academics have it, we are drawn into interactivity with the postmodern text.

Which is why YA novels with a high degree of ambiguity and ambivalence, especially those that are without closure, are so beloved by teachers. With their built-in need for resolution, they are irresistible for discussion and essay assignments. Lois Lowry's *The Giver*, for instance, and Walter Dean Myers's *Monster* have become classics in just a few years, partly because of the inherent pull to resolve their endings. Both, of course, are brilliant pieces of writing with many virtues, but the question that stays with us is whether those colored lights and music at the bottom of the snowy hill are real or a product of Jonas's dying mind and whether Steve's actions have earned his lawyer's perception of him as a "monster." One of the most spectacular unresolved endings in recent years is that of Terry Trueman's *Stuck in Neutral*. Its plot, however, makes it problematic for school assignments—imagine a parent's reaction to "My teacher wants me to write an essay about this book where a kid with cerebral palsy has a father who's maybe going to kill him."

Let me hasten to say that we're not talking here about the kind of unresolved ending that is a setup for a sequel. Cliffhangers have nothing to do with ambiguity, because the reader is not being asked to contemplate several possibilities but to read the next book to find out how the story finally ends. On the other hand, when authors of truly open-ended novels are persuaded by insistent readers to solve the ambiguity with a sequel, the result is seldom valued after the first flurry of excitement. That's because it attempts to take the original story back from us, to negate our partnership in its telling. Lowry's *The Messenger* reveals, albeit rather obliquely, that Jonas survived to become a leader in a more benevolent society. But we still want to go back to puzzling over those mystical colored lights and why the music came from behind as well as in front of the sled. And in spite of its brilliant trapdoors and clever magical misdirection, *Beyond the Chocolate War*, sequel to *The Chocolate War*, was the only one of Cormier's YA novels not to be chosen an ALA Best Book. Jerry as a devotee of passive resistance is no fun at all—we want to continue to agonize over him lying beaten in the Goober's arms and to go on wondering about what Cormier is saying to us with this seeming hero's disconcerting surrender.

It seems to me that in its essence the young adult novel is naturally productive of ambiguity and ambivalence, because the narrator/protagonist is by definition unreliable, limited by the lack of maturity and understanding of adolescence. In that misty mirror, reality can be seen in distorted and ambiguous versions of itself, and the reader must grope for the truth in that inaccurate reflection. The novel told in multiple voices is even more subject to ambiguity, because each speaker adds his or her own perceptions to make the story, and these may contrast and conflict, as in the book that is arguably the prototype of this format, *Making Up Megaboy* by Virginia Walter. An extravagantly ambiguous recent example is *A Fast and Brutal Wing* by Jennifer Jeffries Johnson, in which four voices speak in five formats, and all of them are unreliable for various reasons of hidden agendas or character quirks or visionary insights or mental illness. The reader must compose the true story—or the story that is true for him or her—by making decisions about whom to believe. Another recent book, *Pinned*, by Alfred C. Martino, creates an equally powerful effect more simply, with two strong, clear story lines that collide in a striking ending. One of two things will happen, provoking ambivalence in the reader, who will find his or her sympathies distinctly divided.

No discussion of ambiguity and ambivalence in YA fiction would be complete without at least mentioning David Almond's ineffable novel *Skellig*, in which we are asked to decide who this pale, winged person is that the children have found lying against the back wall of the garage—a madman, an owl-being, the angel of death? Or the playful small puzzles with which Louis Sachar has strewn the landscape of his otherwise straightforward *Holes*. Or Bruce Brooks's *Asylum for Nightface*, a book that echoes the reader's reaction by ending with the words of an onlooker surprised by an ambiguous act: "What the hell—?"

However, there are some readers who don't want to work that hard but who only want to be entertained, to be told a story. Interactivity is not for them; for these readers such literary tricks are a frustrating irritant. Even for an astute critic, gratuitous or excessive ambiguity can be annoying. About a recent YA novel, critic Jonathan Hunt remarked, "I don't like all the unanswered questions at the end of the book. That's not to say I don't appreciate ambiguity. I just don't like feeling cheated to get it. When I read a good ambiguous book, I always feel like it's my fault, like I missed something. I didn't feel that way here. I felt I got everything the author was intending, but that it just didn't add up." Ambiguity has to grow organically from the text, hint at unmentioned but intriguing possibilities. Simply failing to answer the questions raised in the book doesn't create ambiguity, nor does abandoning the effort to reach a coherent conclusion, sometimes because an author is, figuratively, crouched in a corner surrounded by wet paint. That's just plain cheating, at the expense of the reader.

Finally, let me pose a last set of questions to ponder. It should be apparent to anyone that life itself is profoundly ambiguous, and that story is the way we make sense of the buzzing multiplicity of reality, by choosing certain events and relating them to each other in a meaningful pattern. Then why does ambiguity in YA fiction strike us as so artful? Conversely, is the increasing use of ambiguity moving young adult literature closer to being an accurate reflection of the nature of real life? And in the long run, is this a good thing?

Vetting the
Verse Novel

The verse novel? What is it?
It's poetry.

Poetry? What is it?
Who knows.

Maybe Webster knows
Or at least American Heritage.

Aha!
"A composition designed to convey
a vivid and imaginative sense of experience,
characterized by the use of condensed language,
chosen for its sound and suggestive power
as well as its meaning,
and by the use of such literary techniques as
structured meter,
natural cadences,
rhyme,
or metaphor."

Which about sums it up
Except for the part about rhyme.

Originally published in "The Sand in the Oyster," *Horn Book* (September/October 2004):
611–16.

IF YOU THINK THE ABOVE SOUNDS like I've been reading too many YA verse novels, you're right. Twelve, to be exact, of the thirteen or fourteen published so far in 2004. An impressive statistic, because up until last year there had been only about thirty titles in the form's entire ten-year history. But each year more writers have been choosing this way to shape a YA novel, and this year's sudden jump in numbers may mean that the verse novel has become a standard part of young adult literature, rather than an occasional oddity. In any case, we've seen enough now to look at the origins and history, the rules and parameters, the successes and pitfalls of this emerging form.

A long story told in verse is probably the prototype for all literature, but this approach to storytelling faded away with the appearance of the prose novel in the eighteenth century. Its reinvention in YA lit—and *only* in YA lit, because there is no adult equivalent—is one of the glories of adolescent literature. The first verse novel to be recognized as such was the masterwork *Make Lemonade* by Virginia Euwer Wolff, published in 1993. However, the poetry collections of Mel Glenn had been groping toward the form for several years before that. In the late eighties Glenn wrote three books of poems in the voices of his high school students, and in 1991 he assembled those voices around a central theme and place—a guidance counselor's office—in *My Friend's Got This Problem, Mr. Candler*, a book that came within a hair's breadth of being a verse novel. Then in 1996 he got it, with *Who Killed Mr. Chippendale?*

Glenn went on to write four more, while a few other established writers had a try at this new form—Robert Cormier with *Frenchtown Summer*, for example—but often seemingly without any awareness that they were tapping into an emerging literary pattern. Most spoke of the story itself wanting to be told in this manner. Cormier said, "As I began to write it seemed to cry out for verse. I tried writing it in prose but it didn't work, so I let it go its own way." Virginia Euwer Wolff, who had written successful prose novels previously, also seemed surprised by this new shape her words had taken. In an interview with Roger Sutton, she said,

"The form just came to me. . . . I did try changing part of a draft into paragraphs, and I just got all blocked and stifled and couldn't do it." She also wanted the page, with its large amount of white space, to look less intimidating to the young mothers she visualized as her audience.

A handful of new writers, however, jumped into this fresh writing opportunity with awareness and enthusiasm, and some, like Sonya Sones, have continued to be completely committed to it. The verse novel gained mainstream critical acceptance and admission into the classroom when Karen Hesse's *Out of the Dust* won the Newbery Medal in 1998 and further visibility later when Wolff's *True Believer* won the National Book Award and Angela Johnson's *The First Part Last* won the Printz.

But is it poetry? Virginia Wolff, in the face of Roger Sutton's insistence that the compression of her language made it poetry, denied it staunchly. "Writing my prose in funny-shaped lines does not render it poetry," she said. Other authors have agreed with her about their own work. This humility serves them well, because, as Sutton and other critics have agreed, the prevailing pitfall for writers of verse novels is pretentiousness, a self-consciousness about the prosody of their words that can make the whole undertaking seem a little operatic.

Nevertheless, good verse novels fit that dictionary definition of "poetry," especially in their use of condensed language, natural cadences, and metaphor. And as for "a vivid and imaginative sense of experience," I can still feel Billie Jo's burn-constricted hands (in *Out of the Dust*) and smell Jolly's slovenly apartment (in *Make Lemonade*).

But as to structured meter and rhyme, usually the rhythms of ordinary speech take the place of formal metric patterns, and rhyme has not been part of the picture until this year, when Linda Oatman High's sharp and sweet *Sister Slam and the Poetic Motormouth Road Trip* explored the jagged tempo and unexpected rhymes of rap.

The Realm of Possibility by David Levithan is the most innovative verse novel of this year's crop in its playful exploration of poetic form. Levithan uses iambic pentameter ("My girlfriend is in love with Holden Caulfield"), the haiku, the popular song ballad, and probably lots more patterns that I haven't recognized. He even constructs a series of stanzas in which the initial letters of each group follow in alphabetical sequence, and he shapes the whole novel in the circular form of the rondo, and all without losing the authenticity of the voices of the many narrators.

There are several other features that most verse novels share, and that may be definitive for the form. They are almost always written in the present tense and narrated in the first person by a teen. The text is shaped in a succession of one- or two-page poems, usually titled, that end with a punch line. This provides temporary closure for the reader, a necessary resting point in the very concentrated narration. It also provides a way to change speakers often. Some of the best verse novels are told by one voice, but there can be two, three, or multiple voices. A change in speaker is usually indicated in each poem's title or at the beginning of a section as a guide to the shift.

No matter how many speakers there are, they are all intensely internal, focused on the characters' feelings, because emotion is what the verse novel—and poetry—is all about. Characteristically, the action centers on an emotional event, and the rest of the novel deals with the characters' feelings before and after. An example from this year is *Splintering* by Eirann Corrigan, which shows at great length a family's devastation from a home invasion by a drug-crazed intruder. The title of Sonya Sones new work, *One of Those Hideous Books Where the Mother Dies*, is apt (although this particular verse novel is not as grim as it sounds). The death of parents—and grandparents—is a frequent theme because it is the most emotion-causing possibility for the teen years. The effectiveness of the verse novel on this subject is shown beautifully in *North of Everything* by Craig Crist-Evans, in which a boy finds solace for his father's death in the recurring life cycle on a Vermont farm. *Escaping Tornado Season* by Julie Williams also shows a teen coming to terms with a father's death and the disruption his absence causes in her life. Even when a verse novel looks at history, the center is a concentrated emotional event—the Hartford circus fire of 1944 in *Worlds Afire* by Paul Janeczko or the kidnapping of the Lindbergh baby and the subsequent trial and execution of a probably innocent German immigrant in Jen Bryant's *The Trial*.

And in the verse novel there's a whole lot of lovin' going on—not so much sex as the yearning, aching quality of first love that poetry so gracefully captures. *One Night* by Margaret Wild shows first love gone awry, as Helen, a girl with a deformed face, staunchly deals with the pregnancy that is the consequence of one night of what she thought was love. Several of the other verse novels of this year have romantic love as a secondary theme. But the very best, and my personal favorites, are two little books by the Australian poet Steven Herrick. In *Love, Ghosts, & Facial Hair*—prissily retitled from the original *Love, Ghosts, & Nose Hair*—Jack lets go of the ghostly presence of his mother for the love of Annabel. And in *The Simple Gift* Herrick uses spare, ordinary language to tell the exquisitely touching love story of Billy, who at sixteen has chosen to leave his abusive father and become deliberately homeless, and Caitlin, a girl who is looking for some meaning beyond her parents' wealth.

The structure of the verse novel, then, can be quite different from the novel, which is built with rising conflict toward a climax, followed by a denouement. The verse novel is more often like a wheel, with the hub a compelling emotional event, and the narration referring to this event like the spokes. So perhaps the verse novel is not a "novel" at all, or "verse" either, which requires regular meter and rhyme. Is it too late to give this new form another name?

And now, the eternal basic YA question: do the kids like these books? Lynn Evarts, a Wisconsin high school librarian, recently told the YALSA-BK listserv: "Without fail, my kids love the verse novels. It's interesting to watch them and talk with them when they choose one for the first time. Many are hesitant, initially, because they are afraid that it's poetry. I tell them to read a little, and get the feel of the book. . . . To a one, they return raving about them!" But without a watchful librarian to promote books in this funny-looking form, would teens be willing to brave the potential tedium of a story written in what looks like poetry? The jury is still out on this one.

I have to confess that when I open a novel and see those short lines, I often stifle a groan. Sometimes I wonder why the author didn't just *say* it, especially when the poems plonk along over daily events. Why are so many writers turning to verse novels—are they easier to write? Surely not, at least not easier to write *well*, although it cannot be denied that they are shorter. Perhaps the intention of some, like Virginia Euwer Wolff, is to hook reluctant or struggling readers. Or conversely, could it be to make the work seem more "literary" and award worthy? Whatever the reason and the readership, the verse novel is here to stay, and with its condensed language and suggestive power it can make a story soar beyond the possibilities of prose in a way that changes even this reader's initial reluctance to eventual enthusiasm.

The Death of Animals

"THE PETS ARE DEAD MEAT," said horror writer R. L. Stine, talking about his books to a *Time* magazine interviewer in 1993. "If a kid has a pet, he's going to find it dead on the floor." This callous statement from Stine, unfortunately, also applies to more than the horror genre. The degree to which cruelty to animals, particularly dogs, has come to be a stock technique for adding interest in standard young adult fiction is appalling.

True, the death of animals has always been a common denouement in children's literature. Who doesn't remember sobbing over poor abused Ginger in *Black Beauty*, Bambi's bewilderment over the loss of his mother, Charlotte's brave acceptance of the shortness of her life, the sad fate of the Yearling or Old Yeller? These books taught us as children the pleasure of a good cry but also some hard truths about life made bearable by the fact that, after all, Bambi's mother was a deer, and Charlotte was a spider, no matter how lovable they were. But because the animals were presented with compassion and empathy, the pity and terror of their deaths was a catharsis, in the classic literary manner.

No such dignity is allowed the animals who suffer and die in current young adult novels. They are throwaway devices in the plot.

Originally published in "The Sand in the Oyster," *Horn Book* (November/December 1995): 775–82.

The authors give them only enough identity so that our emotions are engaged when the payoff comes, and that moment is frequently full of unnecessarily grisly detail. Too often their torment is used to make a point about a character or a relationship, to symbolize a development in the plot, or simply to add emotional clout to an incident. Such scenes are appearing with more frequency in otherwise excellent young adult novels, despite the possibility that repeated exposure to such fictional gratuitous violence numbs compassion for animal—and by extension, human—suffering.

Although the trend is escalating, animal abuse as a literary trick has been around in young adult fiction since the beginning. In John Donovan's 1969 novel, *I'll Get There, It Better Be Worth the Trip,* a boy's pet dachshund is run over before his eyes after he has been physically affectionate with another boy, thereby fulfilling the then-current unwritten dictum that in a story in which there is homosexual activity, somebody must pay by dying at the end.

Recently, I reread Robert Newton Peck's *A Day No Pigs Would Die,* a novel that has long been upheld as a classic. I found it rambling, unfocused, and full of irrelevant episodes, so much so that I suspect the book's reputation is based solely on the remembered emotion of the scene in which a boy helps his father butcher his pet pig. Not only is that scene ghastly with the details of turning a charming live animal into meat, but its motivation is a fake. The family is poor, true, but not that poor. And while it is logical that a sow who is barren should be butchered, it is not as inevitable as the reader has been led to believe, a point on which the whole plot turns. The book is also distinguished for an especially ugly scene of dog abuse, in which the father and his friend seal a little terrier into a barrel with a weasel, in the interest of "training" the dog. She emerges bleeding and maimed and must be shot.

Z for Zachariah by Robert O'Brien, one of the best post-nuclear holocaust novels, uses the death of a dog in a more integral way than most and with more compassion. Ann Burden thinks she is the last person left on Earth—until Mr. Loomis arrives. When he attempts to make her his slave, she hides in a cave, but he uses her own dog to track her. She realizes with horror that she must shoot the dog.

> I drew the bead; the gun was steady and I could not miss. But at that moment Faro gave a small, impatient tug and a small bark, which came clearly up the hill to my ears. It was his bark of greeting, a soft pleasure bark for me—he knew the cave was just ahead. And at the sound, so gentle and familiar, my finger went limp on the trigger, and I could not do it.

Later, she accepts the inevitable and lays a scent trail across a heavily irradiated river. The dog swims it to reach her and dies that night. Mercifully, O'Brien spares us the details.

In other young adult disaster novels, the killing of dogs is a constant motif. "The dogs were dead," begins chapter six of *Tomorrow, When the War Began* by John Marsden. A foreign army has captured the whole population of a town while they are assembled at an agricultural fair, and the dogs, left chained at home, have died of thirst—or heat exhaustion in closed cars, if their families took them along. Ellie and her band of young people find two of their own dogs alive but later abandon them because they might give away the whereabouts of their hideout by barking. In *Fall-Out* by Gudrun Pausewang a young girl fleeing a nuclear accident sees a man shooting his collie dog, and later one of her friends tells her, "Father killed our two dogs on the second day although he was so fond of them. They would have needed to go out. And who's got several hundredweight of dog food in the house?" Logical. But do we need to know he did it with an axe?

Dog death is often used as a plot device to dramatize just how bad the bad guys are. In Bruce Brooks's *Moves Make the Man*, Bix has always been told that his father was shot by killers who mistook him for someone else. But he has never really believed the story until his mother tells him that they also shot the dog. "It was dead too, beside him," he tells his friend Jerome. "Somehow makes it seem real, you know?"

Chris Crutcher is especially prone to using the death or abuse of animals as a plot device, which is strange, because of all young adult novelists, Crutcher is one of the most compassionate and tender. His work as a child and family therapist has given him great understanding of and insight into human feelings, but his villains are imaginative animal killers. In *Chinese Handcuffs*, Jen is being molested by her stepfather. She tells her boyfriend, Dillon:

> After the first time, he came into my room with a Polaroid picture of my dog's head under his boot, wedged next to the car tire, and told me if I ever told anyone, the dog would have an accident. The day I reported [the abuse] he tied the dog to the back bumper and ran over her and left her on the porch. You couldn't even recognize her face. He ran right over her head.

In *Staying Fat for Sarah Byrnes*, one of the boys in Sarah's therapy circle "was shut up in his closet when he was three years old with his puppy that his stepdad killed. He was there for at least a day but probably it was longer." And in Crutcher's superb novel *Ironman*, he tops that story with an episode in which a disturbed boy's brutal father teaches his son a lesson by shooting the puppy the boy has forgotten to feed. The scene is heartrending, as the boy sits on the front steps cradling the bleeding dog in his lap and blaming himself for its death. But at least we haven't been suckered in by any previous scenes of the cute puppy at play, so most of our sympathy goes to the boy, as Crutcher intends it should. Structurally, the episode works as an exaggerated parallel to the protagonist's struggle with his own father, who also tries to destroy the thing his son loves most "for his own good."

Nor does Crutcher confine himself entirely to dogs. In *Chinese Handcuffs,* Dillon and his brother Preston trap a tough neighborhood cat named Charlie in a gunnysack. "Charlie squirms and fights in the sack like two badgers soaked in hot tar, his voice shrill and powerful, filled with terror and rage." The boys bash the sack against an old wood stove, and

Charlie's pitch changes. He knows at some level where all living things know, that he's going to die, and he's scratching and clawing and screeching to the end. Preston hoists the sack, beats it endlessly against the floor, then loses his grip for an instant. Charlie struggles free. The cat is a mangled, bloody mess, his timbre nearly human.

As the animal crawls across the floor they beat him with a tire iron until he is a twitching ruin, and then throw him into a hastily dug hole behind the garage. In a literary sense, Charlie does not die in vain. Crutcher is too good a writer to waste such drama. He uses the scene as a central and continuing focus in the plot; the guilty secret of this senseless cruelty defines the relationship of the two brothers.

Without a doubt, the most ghastly scene of dog torture in young adult literature is found in Isobelle Carmody's *The Gathering*—a scene so horrifying that I cannot bear to reprise it here, since the book is justifiably long forgotten. There is no literary justification for this detestable spectacle whatsoever; it is simply dumped into the action for a cheap thrill.

So prevalent has animal abuse become in YA fiction that I grow suspicious the moment a dog appears in a book. As the story goes on, if there are increasing appearances by the dog, especially if it is depicted as adorable or faithful or important to one of the characters, I begin to suspect that I am being set up for some dreadful scene. At this point, I lose all interest in finishing the book.

Unfortunately, this reaction taints the reading of a number of fine novels in which the dog is *not* hurt. A recent example is Gary Paulsen's *The Rifle*, a story of a gun crafted during the Revolutionary War and handed down through the generations—still loaded. In the final episode, the rifle, through a series of accidents, goes off and kills a young boy, giving the lie to the slogan, "Guns don't kill people; people kill people." Earlier in the story, when this boy is a child, Paulsen makes a great point of his close relationship with a collie and often gives us the dog's point of view about it. "She would come to love the boy . . . so much she would have laid down her life for him" in "the bond of obligation that connects dogs—and especially collies—to humans." When the boy is older, the dog "spent every waking hour watching him, waiting for him to move so she could be with him."

Immediately the reader smells a setup. Paulsen has already written at least one dog death, albeit a true incident. In his autobiography *Eastern Sun, Winter Moon*, he describes a day from his childhood in the Philippines when he and his beloved puppy were walking on a country road. A truckload of Filipino soldiers roars past, and the driver deliberately swerves to run over the dog. They drive off laughing at the boy's anguish. So it is natural to suspect that *The Rifle* is leading up to at least some heroic doggy self-sacrifice. At the end, when the dog is unharmed but the boy's life is cut short, it is a surprise (and a relief, inappropriate as that reaction may seem).

These are only a few random examples, but any constant reader of YA fiction could probably think of dozens more. It is time for the question to be asked: is it responsible behavior for writers to exploit our affection and concern for animals as an easy way to add emotional charge to a story?

The *Lit* of Chick Lit

As the literary butterfly known as *chick lit* flutters past, let's capture that lepidoptera, pin it to a board, and see what the frivolous and flamboyant creature is all about. Putting metaphors aside, let's discuss how YA chick lit differs from its adult predecessors and other antecedents, define its patterns, respond to some recent press about it, and question its direction and influence.

First, let us acknowledge that the term itself is inherently demeaning, perhaps even sexist. *Chick* is a derogatory term for the presumably empty-headed girls or young women who are both the characters and the readers; *lit* is an ironic reference to the assumed lack of quality writing in the form. Whether any, or all, of so-called chick lit deserves this scorn remains to be seen over time.

The adult prototype, of course, was Helen Fielding's very British and very amusing *Bridget Jones's Diary*. Its success, according to a recent collection of essays (*Chick Lit: The New Woman's Fiction*, edited by Suzanne Ferriss and Mallory Young) and an article in the *New York Times* ("The Chick-Lit Pandemic" by Rachel Donadio), has been followed by imitators all over the world. But these stories of newly independent young women trying to cope with office jobs and the demands of urban pop culture are very different from the teen chick lit that was initiated by the YA Bridget Jones spin-off,

Originally published in "The Sand in the Oyster," *Horn Book* (July/August 2006): 487–91.

Angus, Thongs and Full-Frontal Snogging by Louise Rennison. *Angus* and its sequels, as well as homegrown reads like Meg Cabot's *Princess Diaries* and Ann Brashares's *Sisterhood of the Traveling Pants*, led by a circuitous route to three paperback series that have established the very particular American version of YA chick lit now igniting a wildfire of imitation.

Those three influential paperback series are Gossip Girl by Cecily von Ziegesar, The A-List by Zoey Dean, and The Clique by Lisi Harrison. Each series has sold more than a million copies, according to Naomi Wolf in a wide-eyed and misleadingly titled *New York Times* article, "Young Adult Fiction: Wild Things." Wolf characterizes these books as having a "creepily photorealistic" writing style and "a value system in which meanness rules, parents check out, conformity is everything and stressed-out adult values are presumed to be meaningful to teenagers. . . . The rich are right and good simply by virtue of their wealth." All true enough, as far as it applies to these series. Other markers, too, are characteristic of the paperback YA chick lit style at its worst, often approaching self-parody. Among these are:

detailed descriptions of clothes—which are named by designer and referred to as "outfits";

frequent mention of brand names—"so prominent you wonder if there are product placement deals," says Wolf;

spike heels—the higher the better;

eyeball-rolling—as annoying in the literature as it is in real life;

covers showing body parts but not faces—perhaps reflecting the overwhelming preoccupation with body image;

cell phones, computers, iPods, and other electronic toys—usually to communicate the ongoing story to an absent best friend (and the reader);

exclusive private schools—with such outré courses as "Russian Dissident Indigenous Crafts" and a relaxed attitude toward grades and cutting classes;

casual sex—often in semipublic places like the dressing rooms of fashionable stores;

smoking as an indication of sophistication—an even more repre-
hensible model than the blow jobs, it seems to me;

plentiful booze, but nothing so retro as beer—rather, stylish con-
coctions like chocolate martinis, which are not sipped, but
"swigged" or "gulped," leading to

lots of vomiting—usually on one another's Prada bags or Gucci
boots and often in humiliatingly public circumstances;

the Party—at which there are no adults but lots of alcohol and
drugs and very loud music by named groups and where the best
scenes take place in

the ladies' room—as a venue for malicious gossip, persecution of
nerds, and sex;

and, worst of all,

clunky writing—with unbelievable situations, stereotyped characters, and awkward dialogue.

Against this repellent background moves a plot line glorifying
shallow materialism as the only way to acceptance. Wolf points out
an example in *The Clique*, in which the protagonist "abandons her
world of innocence and integrity . . . to embrace her eventual success as one of the school's elite."

But if Wolf had looked more broadly at the permutations of
chick lit in young adult literature in general and not just paperback
series, she would have seen that in the hands of more skilled and
more responsible writers, a version of chick lit has emerged that is
comparatively benign in its message, even though it may be decorated with some of the markings of the books described above.

At the center of this pattern is a girl who finds herself an outsider at her school, either because she is newly arrived from somewhere else or because of actual physical or social differences. The
school is dominated by the Queen Bitch and her friends, who are
the most cool, the most popular, the most desired. The QB is rich
and beautiful but mean, always ready to tease and torment those
less cool than her and her chosen few. The outsider girl yearns to
be accepted by this powerful in-group, even when she becomes the

target of their jibes. She subverts her own real identity in the effort to fit in with the ruling group, copies their clothes, and accepts their values but eventually (and here is where the pattern differs from Wolf's assumptions about chick lit) becomes disillusioned with them and regains her integrity, often signaled by a reconciliation with a nerdish friend or boy she has previously rejected.

It is important to remember that chick lit novels in general are dramas of social class, not love stories. Even in the books by more nuanced authors, boyfriends are primarily useful as indicators of status—at least until our girl has had her epiphany. A common subplot involves the protagonist's initial rejection of a nice but dorky boy who is a social liability in favor of a dangerous hookup with the QB's boyfriend, a move that backfires with disastrous retaliation from the outraged QB. Designer clothes and electronic toys, too, are not valued for themselves but for their visibility to others as class markers.

This year some excellent YA writers, a few of them familiar names, have played with this archetypal pattern with good results. National Book Award finalist Adele Griffin (*Sons of Liberty*) is not above playing with the motifs of chick lit in *My Almost Epic Summer*, in which Irene's babysitting job at the lake is complicated by gorgeous, self-possessed lifeguard Starla and her wicked blog, as well as both girls' interest in former geek Drew. Lauren Mechling and Laura Moser follow up on the success of their witty *Rise and Fall of a 10th Grade Social Climber* with a sequel, *All Q, No A*, set in a zany New York private school where the girls earn status points for sloppily layered clothes and unkempt hair. Laura and Tom McNeal, in *Crushed*, embed the basic chick lit pattern in a novel that is richly embroidered with some intriguing backstory, engaging characters, and a mystery about a scurrilous underground student tabloid.

The Queen of Cool by Cecil Castellucci turns the pattern inside out with a story of a bored QB who leaves her clique behind when she finds that nerds have more fun. *Hazing Meri Sugarman* and *Meri Strikes Back*, by M. Apostolina, are almost classic in their evocation of the evil in-group headed by a college sorority president so mean that publisher Simon Pulse has started an online fan club to help freshman Cindy get even with her.

This spring has also seen some interesting genre fusion with a chick lit–like verse novel (*The Geography of Girlhood* by Kirsten Smith), a story that meshes chick lit and fantasy (*Golden* by Jennifer Lynn Barnes), and even a throwback to the old "choose your own adventure" format (*What If . . . Everyone Knew Your Name* by Liz Ruckdeschel and Sara James). And *Honey Blonde Chica* by Michele Serros carries chick lit across linguistic borders with a pun on the word *playa*, meaning not *beach* as it does in Spanish, but its street-lingo homograph, *bitch*.

In all of this anatomizing, an important point has gotten lost. Even at its worst, chick lit is *fun*, a fact ignored by solemn critics like me and Naomi Wolf. Yes, the language in these paperback series and other YA books that hew closely to that model is crude—there is plentiful use of the f-word as well as the common vulgarities of everyday speech. And yes, there is sex—lots of it, and often without love or respect. And yes, there is lots of smoking, drinking, and consequent vomiting. And yes, the characters wallow in extravagant spending. But all of this is presented in such an exaggerated way that no sensible teen would take it for anything but the silly wish-fulfillment fantasy it is. And what fun for teens to offer this kick in the pants to adult values, as Roger Sutton acknowledged in a recent *Horn Book* editorial. And what fun for us solemn critics to watch YA lit take this vital, lively, but debased form and transform it into something good and decent, something that reinforces what kids really knew all along: the QB is wrong—nerds win in the end.

Part Three

DEFINING YA

Middle Muddle

BETWEEN CHILDREN'S FICTION AND THE YA NOVEL we are beginning to see the emergence of a particular kind of book aimed at early adolescents, which, for lack of a more specific term, I'll call the middle school novel. Typically these books, like their YA progenitors, focus on the hard problems of growing up but in a way that is softened for the presumed younger readership and with a style that could be characterized as "junior YA." Where exactly is their boundary with young adult fiction? Are there distinguishing differences in subject and treatment?

Nobody at this point has nailed down the answers, although most editors, librarians, and teachers have tentative working definitions of middle school fiction—which differ wildly. By contrast, the young adult novel was immediately perceived from the moment of its inception in 1967 (with the publication of S. E. Hinton's *The Outsiders*) as a different and describable kind of literary animal, and its upper boundary has been clearly differentiated from adult fiction. But the lower end, the middle school novel, has gradually snuck up on us without critical assessment since it burgeoned in the eighties as a spin-off from young adult fiction and as a marketing response to the population bulge of boomers' babies.

Originally published in "The Sand in the Oyster," *Horn Book* (July/August 2000): 483–87.

The kind of book we are trying to define here seems to me to be basically different from the mainstream of children's literature. Books like *Alice in Wonderland, Mary Poppins, Stuart Little,* even *Harry Potter* stem from the great Victorian tradition in that they give a child the illusion of empowerment in a strange but essentially benevolent world. However, in middle school novels, the problems of existing in the real world intrude on the child's life uncomfortably, just as they do in the "new realism" that gave birth to the YA novel. As in YA, the action is centered on the task of growing up, but the middle school novel is distinguished by its gentler tone and focus on prepubescent developmental issues.

So why should defining the middle school novel matter? Such a definition does have pragmatic applications for librarians and teachers—and award committees—in matters of budget and territory. Another practical reason: if middle school novels can be separated out from young adult fiction into their own category, to be shelved and promoted apart, it will free YA from the "contamination" that leads so many teens to reject the whole genre as "baby books." But mostly it matters out of aesthetic playfulness, because an appreciation of form is one of the pleasures of literature.

Searching for measuring tools, I watched myself for a week as I sorted books quickly for YA review. I knew my methods were too superficial, because I have occasionally, to my embarrassment, passed over a book as too young that later becomes a YA favorite. The initial indicators that led me to put a book aside as middle school are the presumed age of the person pictured on the cover, the actual age of the protagonist, the length and thickness of the book, the size of the type, and the amount of white space on the page. Then I took into account whether the author was referred to on the blurb as a writer of books for "children." (Familiarity with an author's previous work is no help, because many cross back and forth, although their books are different on the other side. Robert Cormier, grand master of the YA novel, is quite clear that two of his works are middle school novels: *Other Bells for Us to Ring* and *Tunes for Bears to Dance To.* He admits that he consciously shaped these books for younger readers.) Lastly, I look at the publisher's own age designation—a recommendation I sometimes find unreliable, if not outright laughable.

How do publishers come up with these seemingly arbitrary labels? Looking for some patterns of age definition among publishers, I searched through a stack of this year's catalogs and found only massive confusion about designated age boundaries. According to publishers, a middle or intermediate reader can be anybody between third and ninth grade or eight to fourteen years old or any portion thereof. True, individual books are usually assigned some segment of these years (8–12, 10–14, 9–13), but as boundaries for a genre this is a whale of a huge territory, encompassing a range from young children to almost-adults. There is a puzzling overlap with YA age designations, which can begin as early as ten (but nearly always ends with a hopeful "and up"). The boundaries are confused in other ways, too. It is not unusual for a book to be labeled YA in hardcover but middle school in paper, or vice versa; for one volume in a sequence to slip down into middle school range or up into YA; or for new editions to change age designation. And it is impossible not to notice that intermediate fiction currently outpublishes YA by a ratio of about seven to two, which is puzzling, since the press is full of news about the YA population boom, which we are now entering. One would think publishers would be more savvy about a coming market.

Other sources lay down different age parameters. Ray Barber and Suzanne Manczuk choose the books for their influential "Books in the Middle" column in *VOYA Magazine* specifically for a *middle school* readership. For the purposes of their list, they define middle school as sixth to eighth grade, although they admit that it may begin as low as fifth and as high as ninth grade in different parts of the country, which adds to the general confusion about the literary boundaries as well.

Harcourt editor Karen Grove suggests an innovative and realistic proposal. She feels that there should be three separate categories of readership: ages eight to ten for children's literature, ten to fourteen for books for early adolescence, and fourteen and up for the grittier and more stylistically innovative novels for older teens. But former YALSA president Michael Cart sees books aimed at ten- to fourteen-year-olds as the lower end of YA fiction, not a separate category of their own. "The definition of 'teenager' is clearly expanding and the lines of demarcation are becoming ever increasingly blurred," he wrote on the yalsa-bk listserv. As I talked to editors, writers, and other YA mavens about the middle school novel, I found that the conversation repeatedly veered away from the shape of the literary form to the age and nature of the readership. Scholastic editor Arthur Levine brought it back on target with a challenge: "You have to look at the literature itself if you want to create rules and patterns." Prime examples might be *Bad Girls* by Cynthia Voigt, for the way in which its wickedly irreverent action is limited to the world of the classroom and focuses on the inner workings of friendship, or *Joey Pigza Swallowed the Key* by Jack Gantos for its lighthearted and friendly treatment of a serious behavioral disorder, or this year's Newbery winner, *Bud, Not Buddy* by Christopher Paul Curtis, for the cheerful courage of its protagonist in the face of disastrous situations (the Newbery is nearly always a middle school book).

If the middle school novel can be defined as a literary form, it must first be differentiated from the young adult novel. So let me try to pin down the essence of the latter: the central theme of most YA fiction is becoming an adult, finding the answer to the internal and eternal question, "Who am I and what am I going to do about it?" No matter what events are going on in the book, accomplishing that task is really what the book is about, and in the climactic moment the resolution of the external conflict is linked to a realization for the protagonist that moves toward shaping an adult identity. As Richard Peck has said, "The last page of every YA novel should say not "The End" but "The Beginning."

The middle novel, according to Arthur Levine, deals with a gentler, less self-conscious version of this theme in that it speaks to a young person's practical attempts to find out how the world works. It seems to me that fitting in, or finding a comfortable place in the small world of family and school, is the typical goal of a middle fiction protagonist, while for a YA this venue is to be rejected, or kicked against, in favor of the outside world with all its scary possibilities. The action in a YA is essentially internal, in the turbulent psyche of the adolescent, while the action in a middle book is more external. To illustrate this difference, YA anthologist and educator Donald Gallo suggests a striking comparison between the intermediate Sammy Keyes series by Wendelin Van Draanen and Nancy Werlin's YA novel *The Killer's Cousin*—both mysteries, but one focused externally and the other internally.

Friendships and how they work are important to middle schoolers, and perhaps the quintessential middle school plot centers on an unlikely friendship, as in Rodman Philbrick's *Freak the Mighty*, a story of the powerful alliance between a big dumb boy and his weak but smart friend. Boy/girl relationships, on the other hand, are more innocent in the middle school novel, as in the easy friendship between Jeffrey and Amanda in *Maniac Magee* by Jerry Spinelli; such naïve pairings are out of the question in the often heated atmosphere of YA. Sexuality, of course, is one of the definitive subjects of YA, and the genre allows its expression in ways that are beyond the pale for middle fiction. The same YA permissiveness applies to violence and profanity. There is an edge of anger always just under the surface in most young adult fiction; risky subjects can be explored, and the tone can be very dark. *When She Was Good* by Norma Fox Mazer, for instance, has been both criticized and praised for its unflinchingly grim picture of the devastating mental abuse of a young girl by her pathological older sister. Even darker, *The Copper Elephant* by Adam Rapp makes use of an invented patois in its vivid picture of an overwhelmingly hopeless post-apocalyptic world. The middle school novel may also deal with dark issues like divorce or death, says Karen Grove, but it delves less deeply into the horror of these subjects. A prevailing sunniness even while terrible things are happening is characteristic of the form, as *Bud, Not Buddy* so engagingly illustrates. While YA humor may emerge from between gritted teeth (the protagonists of a number of YA novels actually retreat into angry muteness), an unself-conscious playfulness is one of the most attractive attributes of middle school fiction. And it almost goes without saying that a middle school novel is shorter and simpler in plot and structure than a YA.

Having said all this, I can immediately think of a dozen books that are exceptions to, or fall between, these very tentative outlines of a literary form. *Vanishing* by Bruce Brooks, for example, in which the characters are eleven but speak as if they're eighteen. Or the Redwall series—big, fat, complicated books beloved by kids in the middle. Or *Skellig* by David Almond, which at first glance would seem to be a middle book, despite its selection for a YA Printz Award honor. This deceptively small book uses simple language, and the boy-girl relationship is middle school innocent, yet the story moves into spiritual and aesthetic dimensions beyond the appreciation of the average fifth grader. Does its difficulty make it a YA novel? What about the exceptional fifth grader, who will be entranced by this extraordinary story?

Like most writers, Kathleen Duey, author of Aladdin's American Diaries series, objects to attempts at genre classification. When I asked her to explain why, she replied, "Books awaken, numb, comfort, expose, hurt, heal. Superimposing categories that define to whom books can do these things has to be artificial at best and harmful at worst. I think that the difference is about marketing. Is there profanity? Sex? Graphic violence? If yes, you have YA. Rewrite the same book with the same themes and incidents, but remove these three things, and voilà, you have middle fiction." She added, "Relative simplicity of storytelling structure and language might be a more real definition of the difference."

And so the critic fails in the task. All of the above boils down to only one hard and fast criterion: middle school fiction is not young adult fiction. At this point in its development, middle fiction is still hanging on to the literary coattails of its big brother for its identity (in spite of sales figures). Perhaps this will always be a necessary relationship. Or perhaps in the future, middle school fiction will develop its own canon and distinctive personality out of the rich and confusing range of possibilities it now explores.

Our Side of the Fence

WHERE IS THE BORDER between young adult literature and adult literature? What are the characteristics that define the books that belong on our side of the fence, and why does that border seem permeable only in one direction? Who are the guards who stand at the gates and exchange the currency of one readership and critical standard for the coinage of the other? What about the tourists who try to cross over without learning the language and customs of the other side? Should this wall exist at all, or do its boundaries classify literary identity in an aesthetically useful way?

As we set out to identify the location of that border by defining how young adult literature differs in essence from adult, we are not talking about readership. The question of what young adults read is an entirely separate matter, and one that is perhaps of more practical importance, at least to practitioners of the great art of bringing kids and books together. Teens read some adult novels and nonfiction and children's picture books, graphic novels, and magazines and the backs of cereal boxes, and none of that print matter is necessarily categorized as young adult literature. In this column I am trying to isolate some definitive characteristics of the genre, playing the critic's game of literary form, of shape and standards and what is and isn't a young adult novel. Nor am I even talking about YA

Originally published in "The Sand in the Oyster," *Horn Book* (May/June 2004): 359–62.

appeal. A book can be a dusty shelf-sitter and still undeniably be a young adult novel. Both teen appeal and literary excellence (which may or may not be synonymous) are desirable in the form but not definitive.

A literary genre defines itself by the books that gradually accumulate under its banner, usually initially led by one or two great prototypes, like Tolkien's *Lord of the Rings*, which established the pattern of modern heroic fantasy, or C. S. Forester's Horatio Hornblower series, which set the model for the naval adventure. Or J. D. Salinger's *The Catcher in the Rye*, the prototype for the YA novel, although it was sixteen years ahead of its time.

As the books in an individual genre grow to a body of literature, definitive characteristics of form, voice, and structure begin to emerge, the essential pattern that makes a heroic fantasy, or a naval adventure, or a young adult novel. Scholastic editor Arthur Levine, in a useful statement I have quoted before, says, "You have to look at the literature itself if you want to create rules and patterns." Actually, the critic does not "create" the rules and patterns but points them out in the genre as they already exist.

We might differentiate YA literature from adult by asking these questions: What is a young adult novel? What characteristics are indispensable to its identity, essential for its definition as a YA book? In my thirty-four years of advocacy for young adult literature, I have probably read two or three thousand YA novels, and out of that background it seems to me that certain patterns emerge as definitive.

As I have said in the past in these pages, the central theme of YA fiction is becoming an adult. No matter what events are going on in the book, accomplishing that task is really what the book is about. For example, Graham Salisbury's *Lord of the Deep* is superficially about deep-sea fishing in Hawaiian waters. But the boy's conflicted feelings about his stepfather's morally questionable action can't be resolved until the boy comes to the difficult realization that sometimes a lie is the only mature choice. There is a lot of exciting action centering on catching a big fish, but that isn't what the story is really about. The "rule" illustrated here is that the narration moves swiftly to a point where the protagonist has an epiphany that matures him or her in some vital way and, as a manifestation of that inner change, solves a problem that has been central to the plot. Very occasionally the protagonist may reject the epiphany, which leads to an ending that is ironic or unhappy, but one still within the definition of the form. There is no requirement for hope, or even cheerfulness, in the YA novel.

The central action in YA fiction is essentially internal, in the turbulent psyche of the adolescent (which is why, incidentally, YA novels very rarely make good movies, a form that is inherently told from the third person). However, this internal action must not be a contemplative monologue but embedded in straightforward external action. Voice is all-important here and is the quality that most clearly distinguishes YA from adult fiction. In *The Catcher in the Rye* we first hear that self-absorbed, angry, and touchingly vulnerable voice of the One True Outsider and see the adult world through Holden Caulfield's limited but judgmental perception, a viewpoint that seems to me to be seminal to the form. Whether it is told in first or third (or even second) person, to be a YA novel a book must have a teen protagonist speaking from an adolescent point of view, with all the limitations of understanding this implies. An adult novel may have a teenage protagonist, but the action is seen from the vantage point of adult memory looking back, a perspective the reader is presumed to share. As Richard Peck once said about Carson McCullers's *A Member of the Wedding*, "It wasn't written for the young, of course. It was for readers who'd made a safe passage to adulthood and dared to look back." By contrast, a YA novel is told from within the confines of a lack of maturity that is inherent in being a teenager, particularized to a character.

To be a YA novel, then, a book must have a climactic epiphany of new maturity as the subtext and be told in the YA voice from the limited adolescent viewpoint. In addition, it must be relevant to the lives of young readers in some way. Disqualifiers, it seems to me, would be settings or subjects outside the scope or interest of contemporary teens and long passages in the voice of an adult or a child character. Within these parameters a freedom to experiment has led to an enormous range of tone and style.

Why is it necessary to get so complicated about what is and isn't YA? Don't publishers designate their books by age level, and isn't that enough? No, it's not. Any book that comes from the juvenile division of a publishing house and is marked "twelve and up," or "fourteen and up" can usually be assumed to be YA rather than adult, although these publisher-guardians of the borders are sometimes dead wrong in their labeling. The Printz Award Committee takes this publisher age designation as its criteria, and, in my opinion, this has led to some misjudgments. Laying aside considerations of literary quality, at least two of the recent winners seem to me to be adult novels masquerading under the publishers' YA label. *A Step from Heaven* by An Na opens with a long section from the perspective of a child and seems to me to lack a clear epiphany at the end. *Postcards from No Man's Land* by Aidan Chambers has many passages told by adults where adult concerns fuel the action and the teenage protagonist is offstage. Neither can teens be assumed to bring empathy and historical understanding to the many adult World War II memoirs that bog down the center of the book.

The reverse situation occurs more often—young adult novels that for some obscure marketing purpose have been issued from the adult side of the house, thus being in danger of missing their natural readership. A striking example is *The Perks of Being a Wallflower* by Stephen Chbosky, surely a YA novel by anybody's definition, but published by Simon & Schuster's adult division. In the past, this strategy sometimes indicated a YA novel that the publishers deemed too hot to handle for the young adult market, usually because of sexual content. Judy Blume's *Forever* is a prime example. Or it could also be that the publisher feels that the book will sell more copies, even to teens, as an adult title. A third possibility for blurring the borders is the "crossover" promotion extended to both adult and teen audiences for a few exceptional books edited on the juvenile side of the house, with the intention of extending their readership beyond the tight limits of the young adult market. Sometimes this works and sometimes it doesn't. *Fade* was an early crossover attempt to broaden Robert Cormier's recognition, but it had very little effect on the public's perception of him as a children's author, in spite of the fact that the book was reviewed as an adult title in the *San Francisco Chronicle*, the *Washington Post Book World*, and the *New York Times Book Review*. In recent years, however, Philip Pullman's His Dark Materials trilogy was a successful crossover, and the trend seems to be growing.

A related phenomenon was the much publicized attempt in 2002 by a number of well-known adult authors—among them Clive Barker, Joyce Carol Oates, Michael Chabon, and Isabel Allende—to traverse the boundary to the young adult world. Not all of these tourists in YA territory grasped the requirements of the form, and although they are all acclaimed as fine writers in their own territory, not all their young adult novels were equal to the level of excellence already established by the YA canon.

And the fact remains that it is infinitely more difficult for authors (and books) to cross the border in the other direction. The literary establishment has not been willing to give even the best young adult writers the recognition and respect they would need to cross over into the wider audience and more lucrative world of adult literature, assuming any of them might want to make the shift.

There are many larger questions about the implications of these labels and boundaries, but simply pinning down the shape of the YA genre will have to be enough for now. As a critic, an important part of my job is to define literary structure, because a pure appreciation of form points the way, provides the standards, and is one of the great pleasures of literature.

Smash/Crash/Slash

"BOOKS FALL OPEN. YOU FALL IN." These opening lines of David Mc-Cord's poem are a delightful vision and an experience that all we book lovers have had at times in our reading lives.

So now that I've tipped my hat to the wonderfully evocative theme of this conference, I want to narrow it down to one particularly interesting—and sometimes alarming—aspect of young adult literature.

Last summer I was asked to write an article on violence in literature for children and young adults for a new Scribner encyclopedia of violence in America. As I got into the research and discussed the subject with colleagues, I had some interesting revelations and came up with what I think are some intriguing theories.

First, let's acknowledge that violence has always been a component of literature, from Homer's heroes slashing through the Trojan Wars, to Oedipus gouging out his eyes with his mother's brooch, to Hamlet strewing the stage with corpses, and on to the latest adult bestseller. But violence in literature for kids is a topic that brings out some strong reactions in many folks.

The fact is, we simply do not know if reading about violence is good or bad for young people. There is no empirical data on the

Based on a talk given at the Young Adult Conference, Sam Houston State University, Huntsville, Texas, November 1, 1997.

effects of *reading* violent scenes in fiction. Sure, there have been literally thousands of studies of the effects of viewing violence on television and film, but none on reading, as far as I could determine. We can extrapolate from the studies of television and film, which almost universally show that viewing violence raises the level of aggressive behavior, at least for a period immediately following the experiment. But the active experience of reading is in many ways quite different from the passive experience of television viewing, and so the effects, too, may be quite different.

Another crucial dissimilarity is in the responsible way violence is portrayed in realistic young adult fiction, as contrasted with the gratuitous mayhem on television. In television and film the violent act is up close and in your face. It just happens, and the story goes on in other directions. The aftermath of violent acts is seldom of interest. But in YA novels the violent act is seen as a bad, abnormal action, and it often takes place offstage or before the story starts. The protagonist is nearly always the victim of the violence, not the perpetrator. The emphasis and the whole focus of the narrative is on the consequences and on strategies for survival and healing. (We're talking now in the context of realistic YA fiction. Mysteries, fantasy, sci fi, and horror are something else, and we'll get to them later.)

As I thought about this, I realized that strongly held opinions about violence in kid's books can take the form of four conflicting attitudes, which lead to confusion and controversy. So let's sort out those four attitudes.

First, there are people who take the position that viewing or reading about violence is a healthy catharsis. They argue that violent impulses are inborn, instinctive human behavior, and so it is good to release the buildup of those impulses through vicarious violent experiences, like watching aggressive sports or viewing films where cars crash and things blow up. This theory, in a more Freudian but gentler form, was applied to the violence in fairy tales by Bruno Bettelheim in his landmark book, *The Uses of Enchantment.* Bettelheim maintained that because fairy tales have been handed down through the oral tradition for hundreds of years, they have come to be symbolic renderings of unconscious feelings and transitional life experiences. So the bloody swords and wicked witches in fairy tales are beneficial and useful to children, he said, because they help them deal with their own chaotic, anxious, and angry fantasies.

Second, there are many child and young adult advocates who feel that kids are vulnerable and tender and so should be shielded from knowledge of the violence in the world around them until they are old enough to handle it. Whether this attitude is invoked depends a lot on the age of the child and the kind and degree of the violence.

Third, opponents of this protectionist position insist that writers for children and especially young adults have an obligation to tell the truth about the pervasiveness of violence in the world and to provide the information that will help young readers learn to cope with it.

And fourth are those cheerful souls who say that books with lots of violence in them are harmless fun, because it's all just make-believe and kids know the difference from real life.

Confusingly, not only do these attitudes conflict, but you'll hear all four of them used in the same discussion, sometimes by the same people about the same book, and no one of these attitudes covers all cases.

Let's take a look at the forms violence takes in YA fiction, and as we go along, decide in your own mind which of these four attitudes you would take toward each type.

We'll start with a kind of literary violence that I find particularly distressing—cruelty toward animals. You all remember, I'm sure, sobbing over the death of Charlotte or Bambi's mother when you were little children. In YA fiction the violent death of an animal is sometimes the means of the protagonist's coming of age, or threatened harm to dogs or cats or horses is frequently used to build suspense or simply to engage the reader's emotions. This tendency has gotten out of hand lately, as I said in a *Horn Book* column last year ("The Death of Animals"), with books in which a cat in a sack is battered to death, or a dog is doused with gasoline and set on fire.

Turning now to violence among humans, the realistic young adult novel by its very nature is a form that welcomes violence. The genre originated, remember, with a story of gang warfare, *The Outsiders*, and soon became known as the "new realism" for its fictional portrayals of gritty social and personal problems. Exploring these problems, by necessity, often involved violent images. But this violent action, which usually took place offstage, functioned in the plot as the motivating force for the young protagonist to gain maturity by overcoming its consequences. This is still true of YA fiction.

Violence within the family is one of the most common themes in young adult novels. It usually takes the form of an abusive parent, stepparent, or older sibling. Sexual abuse of a young person by an adult, related or not, abounds in YA fiction, as in the devastating pages of *Living Dead Girl* by Elizabeth Scott.

Suicide is the third leading cause of death among high school students, and so it is appropriate that it should be the subject of a number of YA novels, most recently *Thirteen Reasons Why* by Jay Asher. The emphasis in these books is on the aftermath for those who are left behind. The grieving process after the violent death of a parent is a similar theme.

Homicide is a daily reality in many parts of American society, and so essential learning for many teens is the healing process for survivors of murder, assault. or the violent accidental death of friends.

Sports as a venue for acting out violent impulses is a frequent theme in young adult literature, often centering on the figure of a brutal coach or a frustrated father as provocateur.

And then there is the ubiquitous bully, a staple of YA lit forever.

Social violence resulting from the pressures of poverty, racial discrimination, or other dysfunctions of society is on a different level. In this type of YA novel the blame is more diffuse, and the solution must compromise with the existing state of the world.

Sexual assault is an especially ugly symptom of social unrest, and it has frequently appeared in young adult literature, often in the form of acquaintance rape, as in *Speak* by Laurie Halse Anderson.

"Gay bashing" in various degrees of violence is also often a component of YA plots.

Guns are both fascinating and frightening to teens with good reason, even beyond the Columbine shootings: one out of every four teenage deaths is caused by a gun. Several YA authors have explored this fatal attraction in compelling novels.

Political violence is even farther removed from the victim's control, and YA literature has not shrunk from exploring some of the worst violent injustices of the past—or the present. Most visible has been social injustice against African Americans, a subject for YA fiction that could be its own ten-page bibliography, from Harper Lee's *To Kill a Mockingbird* to Chris Crowe's *Mississippi Trial 1955*.

War, of course, is the ultimate political violence. Since it is mostly young men in their late teens who fight wars, fiction about it should be of vital importance to young adults. Interestingly, there is no glory in YA novels about battle; instead they are full of the suffering and madness of war. Two classics are *The Last Mission* by Harry Mazer and *Fallen Angels* by Walter Dean Myers.

The Jewish Holocaust of World War II, of course, is violence gone mad, and it is important that young people learn about *these* horrors to prevent them from ever happening again. A number of fine memoirs and novels on this subject have been penned for teen reading.

So much for the realistic YA novel. Now let's look at violence in a different kind of book: fantasy and science fiction and their relatives. We begin with a subgenre that bridges the gap between the two styles of literature, a kind of story I like to call "lethal pursuit." The prototype is Robb White's *Deathwatch*, but Suzanne Collins's *The Hunger Games* is the most recent example of this breathless type. In these stories the protagonists are being chased by somebody who wants to do them harm. There are thrilling escapes and ambushes and narrow squeaks. But it is the constant threat of violence that gives these stories their tingle of excitement. The plot is like a game, and therefore readers can see that the violence is not meant to be believed on the level of, say, the violence in a story about an abusive parent. This is true of most thrillers. Mysteries are even more like formal games, and the murders are just part of the ritual moves.

Fantasies have even more room for creative violence. Think of the vampire's bloody kiss, for instance, or the werewolf's bite. Heroic fantasy, starting with *The Lord of the Rings*, is inherently violent because of its structure, as the plucky little band of good folks, led by the protagonist and a magic talisman, struggle onward in their journey toward the ultimate battle between good and evil. There are lots of fierce encounters and skirmishes on the way, and the violence is often colorful and inventive. But this has mostly been acceptable to guardians of juvenile morals, because the situations are by definition unreal, so the violence is seen as part of the fun and excitement of the story.

However, the limit of tolerance for fantasy violence was reached in the nineties when the phenomenon of the horror paperback series began to show enormous popularity with teen readers, and even—with the advent of R. L. Stine's *Goosebumps*—small children. These loathsome books, with their ludicrous plots and cardboard characters, were certainly not literature, but young people devoured them voraciously. Some adults were alarmed by the welter of bloody and nauseating scenes in these books, but others were willing to overlook the nastiness because "at least they're reading." Hostilities broke out in the form of articles in magazines and newspapers, television news coverage, and censorship attempts in schools and libraries, while young people continued to demand more and more grisly horror. Eventually the craze ran its course, as most fads in YA lit do.

About now, those of you who know my work may be beginning to think, "What about Robert Cormier? You haven't even *mentioned* Cormier." Well, I thought about it—a lot—but I finally decided that the violence in Cormier's work (and there *are* a lot of memorable instances, I admit) is outside of this discussion. Cormier is unique, I think, in his total immersion in the theme of ultimate evil and the ability of the human spirit to transcend it. The occasional

violent acts in his books are shocking only in retrospect, because
when you read them in context, they blend into the darkness like
black spots set against a black wall. What Brint or Artkin or Archie
Costello *do* is not as appalling as who they *are*.

There are a number of other aspects of this subject that I could
have opened up here if we had time. For instance: Do boys like
violent stories more than girls do? Is sexuality linked with violence
in horror fiction? Why do kids like to read about violence? What
criteria could we use to judge whether violence is acceptable in a
particular novel?

Clearly we need to expand our thinking about this matter,
and we need some serious research for guidance. Now I know I've
raised more questions here than answers—but that's the way it is
with young adults and young adult literature, isn't it? There are no
comfortable, one-size-fits-all answers. It all depends—on who is
doing the writing, on who is doing the reading, and on who is bringing them together.

A Loving Farewell to Robert Cormier

YOUNG ADULT LITERATURE HAS LOST ITS GRAND MASTER. On November 2, 2000, Robert Cormier died in Boston after a brief illness. He was seventy-five years old, but his thirteen YA novels speak to the hearts of teens everywhere and will continue to do so for many years to come. Cormier was acknowledged as the finest writer of the genre—and also the first to show the literary world that YA novels could be not only realistic about teen concerns, but unflinchingly honest about the big questions like the abuse of power, courage, forgiveness and redemption, and the struggle to stay human in a world that is, as C. S. Lewis has said, "enemy-occupied territory." While the daring of his subjects has often drawn censorship attack, the brilliance of his writing earned him many literary prizes and places on honor lists. He was the recipient of the American Library Association's Margaret Edwards Award in 1991 and the ALAN Award of the National Council of Teachers of English in 1982, both given for lifetime achievement in young adult literature, as well as many other honors, both national and international.

The publication in 1974 of Cormier's first YA novel, *The Chocolate War*, initiated a new level of literary excellence in the fledgling genre of young adult fiction. It also began a storm of controversy about the darkness and hard truth-telling of his work that continues

Originally published in *Horn Book* (March/April 2001): 245–48.

to this day. The critical dialogue generated by *The Chocolate War* led to recognition not only of Cormier's gifts but also of the young adult novel by the literary establishment. As critic and YA author Michael Cart said in the *Los Angeles Times*, Cormier "singlehand-edly . . . transformed young adult literature." *The Chocolate War* has become a classic, a staple of the high school English curriculum. Yet would-be censors, perhaps troubled by its darkness and uncompromising ending, continue to attempt to ban it on unfounded grounds of explicit sexuality and excessive profanity. In a list compiled by the American Library Association of the most frequently challenged books of the past decade, *The Chocolate War* is number four.

After the success of his first YA novel, in 1977 Cormier astounded critics with the brilliantly constructed psychological thriller *I Am the Cheese*. The story moves on three different levels that are intricately braided together, raising many questions that are not resolved until the very end when the carefully created illusion, an entire false plot, is suddenly swept away to reveal a completely unsuspected (but logically constructed) reality. In the following years, Cormier continued to surprise his readers with the originality of each new book while maintaining a continuity of recognizable style and themes that came to be called *cormieresque*: short cinematic scenes, taut dialogue, a deceptively straightforward story undergirded by intricate structure and layers of tricky allusion and metaphor, an intense focus on the emotion of the situation, and a dark awareness of evil as an implacable obstacle in human affairs. *After the First Death* (1979) compares the terrible naïveté of a young terrorist with an army general's fanatical patriotism in a novel shimmering with built-in puzzles and trapdoors. A volume of short stories, *Eight Plus One* (1980), was followed by the stark experimental hospital setting and soaring ending of *The Bumblebee Flies Anyway* (1983); the eagerly awaited sequel *Beyond the Chocolate War* (1985) used the magician's trick of misdirection for some surprising effects and intriguing character twists. *Fade* (1988) broke new ground for Cormier with its sprawling three-part story that bordered on science fiction—the tale of a boy cursed with the hereditary ability to make himself invisible. It opens with a gentle autobiographical coming-of-age story drawn from Cormier's own French-Canadian background, shifts into a brittle Manhattan-set examination of the nature of fiction and reality, and ends with a horror fantasy.

Readers had barely gotten their bearings after this unsettling blend of truth and wild imagination when Cormier surprised them once again with his gentlest (and least known) novel, *Other Bells for Us to Ring* (1990), a story of eleven-year-old Darcy, who is both attracted to and terrified by the Catholicism of her friend Kathleen Mary, and who is desperate for a miracle to bring her father back from World War II. The story is unusual for Cormier in that its protagonist is a girl and the intended audience is middle school readers. *Tunes for Bears to Dance To* (1992) was also aimed at this younger readership, but in *We All Fall Down* (1991) and *In the Middle of the Night* (1995) Cormier returned to a more mature exploration of themes of guilt and salvation and love denied. Many reviewers found *Tenderness* (1997) profoundly disturbing in its ultimately sympathetic portrayal of a young serial killer, but it remains one of Cormier's most popular books with teens. *Heroes* (1998) is told by the (literally) faceless Francis Joseph Cassavant, who has returned from WWII to Cormier's fictional hometown of Monument to take revenge on both himself and his sweetheart's rapist. And Cormier once again shook up his readers' expectations with a fresh new direction in his most recent book, the autobiographical verse novel *Frenchtown Summer* (1999), told in a series of evocative and poignant short poems. A final novel, with the working title "The Rag and Bone Shop" was nearly complete at his death and may be published next year.

The contrast between Robert Cormier's dark novels and the sunny and kindly nature of the man himself was always a revelation to fans meeting him for the first time. He lived a life of great stability and contentment, growing up in a large, warm French-Canadian and Irish-American family in the small mill town of Leominster, Massachusetts (the real-life Monument); marrying Constance Senay, the girl of his dreams; working as a newspaper man for many years and writing fiction on weekends in the midst of his noisy family of four growing children. Not until he was almost fifty did he find success as a young adult writer, with the help of his agent

Marilyn Marlow. Although Cormier suffered from shyness and bullies during his own adolescence, he never deliberately set out to address these issues by writing for teens. He often said, "I've aimed for the intelligent reader and have often found that that reader is fourteen years old." His young readers were important to him, and he wrote long personal replies to the hundreds of letters he received from young fans. One of the worst-kept secrets of YA fiction has been that Cormier embedded his own phone number in *I Am the Cheese,* and young fans who discovered that fact and dared to call him up always found a sympathetic listener.

Those who knew Cormier, and even those who met him casually, were overwhelmed by his simple goodness. He cared about people, and though he was never physically robust, he gave away his time and energy unstintingly—traveling and speaking to august literary assemblies as well as to awestruck kids in libraries and small-town school boards under censorship fire; giving interviews to anybody who asked; counseling new writers; and talking for hours to teens who called him on the phone. This world-renowned writer spent the last spring of his life writing a history of the parish as a gift for St. Cecilia's Church, where he had been educated by nuns and had worshipped all his life.

Robert Cormier loved his young readers, and he loved his work. Last year I interviewed Bob once again and asked him, "In your writing career, have you accomplished what you set out to do in the beginning?" He answered with characteristic humility: "Oh, yes. My dream was to be known as a writer and to be able to produce at least one book that would be read by people. That dream came true with the publication of my first novel—and all the rest has been a sweet bonus. All I've ever wanted to do, really, was write."

That writing has left us a legacy of wonderful books, a body of work that will endure. But more—those of us who were lucky enough to have been his friends will always feel blessed. So while we grieve for his passing, let us at the same time celebrate the life of this great good man and give thanks for the way his work has disturbed the universe.

Researching YA in the Elysian Fields

THE KERLAN. A NAME INVOKED in hushed tones by devotees of children's and young adult literature. A sort of heaven where manuscripts of the books we love go to be preserved forever. A collection of 100,000 books, as well as 16,000 files of holographs, typescripts, page proofs, artwork, editorial letters, and other assorted contents of authors' office closets. Official title: The Kerlan Collection of Children's Literature, part of the Children's Literature Research Collections at the University of Minnesota.

Okay, but what's in it for *young adult* literature advocates? How much of this mighty collection relates to books for teens, and what can researchers in that genre discover there? Checking out the website (http://special.lib.umn.edu/circ/) and perusing the online catalog, I find that although the collection's declared focus is children's literature, a number of familiar YA writers appear to be represented. I spot some omissions (Avi, Joan Bauer, Virginia Euwer Wolff), and when I use "Finding Aids" to check the contents of individual author files, I discover that some writers I think of as YA (Richard Peck, Jane Yolen) have donated mostly their *children's* titles to the Kerlan. Still, there is enough enticing young adult material in the online catalog to motivate me to book

Originally published in "The Sand in the Oyster," *Horn Book* (January/February 2007): 101–6.

an investigative flight to Minneapolis and plan a visit with the help of the collection's curator, Karen Hoyle.

The campus of the University of Minnesota is huge. There are miles of square, matter-of-fact, red-brick buildings, the Mississippi River, and one utterly outrageous metal-clad building by Frank Gehry. Finding the Kerlan's offices in the Andersen Library, I am welcomed warmly into the large, well-lighted workroom by Curator Hoyle, who emerges from among the congestion of files and book trucks in a sturdy librarian's work apron. Mozart is playing softly in the background, and staff are working busily at their desks. Hoyle assigns me a locked cupboard to store everything I have brought along—standard security procedure, not so much for the safeguarding of my belongings as for the protection of the rare documents housed here.

Hoyle fills me in on the background of the collection. It was established in the 1940s by University of Minnesota alumnus Dr. Irvin Kerlan, former chief of medical research for the U.S. Food and Drug Administration. He collected rare children's books as a hobby, acquiring the best books published each year along with classics and past Newbery winners. Later he also pursued background material and original manuscripts and organized exhibitions of his collection for libraries and art galleries all over the world. In 1949 he made arrangements with the university to house his collection, and after his death in 1963 a staff was provided to supervise further development of the archive. Karen Hoyle has been the curator since 1967 and has built not only an expanding collection, but an extensive program of exhibits, speakers, awards, loan portfolios for schools, scholarships for researchers, and a very active Kerlan Friends organization.

At Hoyle's suggestion, I had sorted through the catalog at home and requested the files on twenty-four YA authors, giving preference to those that seemed to have promising amounts of correspondence or corrected early manuscripts. When I am ushered into the glass-enclosed reading room, those files await me—four book trucks stacked with fifty-six file boxes, assembled by library assistant Meredith Gillies, a willing and helpful aide during my stay. It's clearly too much of a good thing for the three days I have available, but I thank her and happily carry the first box to my table.

The boxes are filled with meticulously indexed manila folders that contain the manuscripts. My first discovery is a disappointment: many of the files contain only clean final typescripts, or page proofs, nearly identical in text to the printed book. All those early mistakes and wrong turns that are so revealing of the writing process have been spirited away by the delete key, leaving only the finished work.

However, I persevere and soon hit pay dirt. In the Gary Paulsen boxes I find several partial manuscripts of *Caught by the Sea* that are heavy with the editor's penciled comments. A close examination of these notes shows that the editor worked with Paulsen's trademark style to make it even more clipped and direct—sentences are shortened, syntax is simplified. A close look at the editing on another nonfiction Paulsen title, *Guts*, is also interesting, especially the juicy fact that the original title—which thankfully didn't survive—was "Eating Eyeballs and Guts." The editor deletes Paulsen's occasional brief irrelevant memories or anecdotes, often introduced with phrases like "I was to find later that. . . ." The effect is to accomplish the author's stated goal of making the background that went into the writing of *Hatchet* immediate and personal to the reader. However, a first draft of *Soldier's Heart*, a book to which Paulsen brought strong commitment and inspiration, shows only minimal editorial change.

I move on to find a treasure—the four-year correspondence between Chris Lynch and editor Ginee Seo that shaped the remarkable YA novel *Inexcusable*. This material is just waiting for a dissertation. Seo's long letters of critical analysis, her questions clarifying characters and motivations, are too good to be hidden away in the archives. And her letters are covered with Lynch's handwritten reactions and his plans for changes. The whole exchange is an example of the writer/editor partnership at its best.

In occasional files I notice a thread of editorial struggle with those pesky f- and s-words. Several editors wonder if the awkwardness of asking the author to clean up the language is worth the increased likelihood of school use. This evidence of a perennial debate alerts me to a gap in the otherwise excellent access to the collection and one that could form the basis for a future project. Although there is a two-volume book index of authors, titles, editors, and subjects (*The Kerlan Collection: Manuscripts and Illustrations*), subject access through this and the online checklist is limited to the major topics of the books themselves, not the editorial content of the files. Researchers looking for letters from teens, discussions of age suitability, or specific topics such as censorship must depend on their knowledge of the field to guide them to the most likely author files in which to find that material.

I tear myself away from these fascinating explorations when a young student staffer, Marit McCluske, comes to show me the Kerlan stacks, an archive eighty-two feet underground that the staff calls "The Cavern." Aptly named, I find, when we descend into the vast, cold concrete space. Here on the lower of two levels, the file-crammed stacks soar fifty feet high and the upper shelves must be reached by a motorized cherry picker driven by a certified driver or, in a pinch, a scary climb on a tall metal ladder. Double walls insulate the rooms, in which temperature and humidity are carefully controlled to preserve the files and 100,000 books.

Back in the warm reading room, I plunge into the boxes and boxes of files on the making of Lois Lowry's *The Giver*. Here I am amused to see her three editors struggling with Lowry's deliciously ambiguous ending. Again and again they try to spell out to themselves and to each other what it could mean, and again and again they plead for clarification from the author, only to have her persist with her original and utterly right ambiguity almost without change. She even adds a few lines to the last chapter in the final galley so her concluding words will appear in the most effective placement on the printed page. Other notes from the editors and from Lowry to herself focus on moving the writing toward consistency in this imagined world ("delete all references to love"). An additional file of letters documents a particularly naïve censorship challenge, in which some parents seemed to think that Lowry was offering the dystopia she had created as an ideal world.

I search further and discover another rich archive in the correspondence generated by Marion Dane Bauer in creating *Am I Blue?* her landmark anthology of gay and lesbian short stories. Chatty letters to and from contributors, and also from writers reluctantly turning Bauer down, reveal the evolution of the work from an insider's point of view. A particularly interesting angle is that the book was originally contracted by Delacorte editor David Gale, who shortly thereafter moved to HarperCollins, whereupon Delacorte editor-in-chief Craig Virden graciously allowed Bauer to cancel her contract and move to Harper with Gale. And a year after James Cross Giblin, Bauer's usual editor at Clarion, had turned down the book because he felt it wouldn't sell, the files show him submitting a short story for the anthology. There are also many letters from gay and lesbian teens thanking Bauer for the support her book gave them.

For the first two days I have the whole reading room to myself, although there are volunteers from Kerlan Friends working away at indexing and filing to make the collection more accessible. But on the third day a young woman and her retired librarian mother come simply to enjoy the glories of the Kerlan. They sit at the next table wearing the obligatory white gloves required for turning the pages of the collection's most impressive holding—the original India ink drawings by Wanda Gag for *Millions of Cats.* Visitors, graduate students, classes, and scholars who come to use the collection are listed in the Kerlan newsletter, and there seems to be a steady stream of them, if not a rushing river; the staff also fields brief reference questions over the phone or through e-mail.

In the files for Nancy Garden's *The Year They Banned the Books,* I encounter the inevitable difficulty of researching original manuscripts. Both the manuscript and editor Margaret Ferguson's letters to Garden are interspersed with many small paragraphs in tiny blue script in a maddeningly illegible hand. My curiosity outweighs my frustration, though, and I uncover cryptic notes like "instructions to self," lists of which characters are sitting in which classes at a given time, and monologues by those characters, evidently written just for practice.

But the archive for Harry Mazer's *The Last Mission* is a satisfying feast. Here I find pages and pages of notes containing the author's memories of the World War II bombing raid and plane crash that was the basis for the novel, detailed drawings and notes for a cover that was never used, and several stream-of-consciousness musings on the theme of war. "What is my conviction about this book?" he asks himself. Equally fascinating is the correspondence between Mazer and other veterans that followed the publication of his story in *8th Air Force News*. One former flyer writes, breathtakingly, "Our plane was directly in back of yours. We saw you go down."

My time is up. I reluctantly close the last file box, hoping fervently that the Kerlan will come to be a final resting place for more YA manuscripts (the messier the better) and that many more students and scholars will flock to this literary nirvana to document the movement and meaning of young adult literature.

Part Four

FIRST LOOKS AT MASTERWORKS

The Gift of *The Giver*

ONCE IN A LONG WHILE a book comes along that takes hardened young adult reviewers by surprise, a book so unlike what has gone before, so rich in levels of meaning, so daring in complexity of symbol and metaphor, so challenging in the ambiguity of its conclusion, that we are left with all our neat little everyday categories and judgments hanging useless. Books like Robert Cormier's *I Am the Cheese* or Terry Davis's *Mysterious Ways* are examples of these rare treasures. But after the smoke of our personal enthusiasm has cleared, we are left with uneasy thoughts. Will young adults understand it? Will the intricate subtleties that so delight us as adult critics go right over their heads? Will the questions posed by the ending leave them puzzled and annoyed, rather than thoughtful and intrigued? It all depends—on the maturity of the particular young adult, on how well we introduce the book and follow up with discussion, and on certain qualities in the book itself. In the past year young adult literature has been blessed with such an extraordinary work: *The Giver* by Lois Lowry.

The Giver is particularly surprising because it is a major departure from the style and type of book we have come to expect from Lois Lowry, as *Horn Book* editor Anita Silvey pointed out in her

Originally published in "The Sand in the Oyster," *Horn Book* (November/December 1993): 717–21.

July/August 1993 editorial. Up until now, much of Lowry's work has consisted of "contemporary novels with engaging characters that explore something very rare—a functional family." But *The Giver* is a dystopia, "driven by plot and philosophy—not by character and dialogue," and the picture of the functional family turns disturbingly awry as the story proceeds. Indeed, it is Lowry's skill at depicting cheerful, ordinary reality that makes the revelation of the sinister difference in this alternate reality so chilling.

Most surprising of all is the leap forward Lowry has made in mastering the creation of a subtext by innuendo, foreshadowing, and resonance. Take, for example, the opening sentence. "It was almost December, and Jonas was beginning to be frightened." The word *December* is loaded with resonance: the darkness of the solstice, endings, Christmas, cold. *Almost* and *beginning* pull forward to the future source of his fear, "that deep, sickening feeling of something terrible about to happen." The name Jonas, too, is evocative—of the biblical Jonah, he who is sent by God to cry against the wickedness of Nineveh, an unwilling lone messenger with a mission that will be received with hostility. In one seemingly simple sentence Lowry sets the mood and direction of her story, foreshadows its outcome, and plants an irresistible narrative pull.

The fascinating gradual revelation of a world and its interlocking rationale as explained by a protagonist immersed in the culture is reminiscent of Margaret Atwood's *The Handmaid's Tale*. Lowry plays with our perceptions and our emotions, creating tension by presenting details of this community that win our approval and then hinting at something terribly wrong. The family, for instance, seems ideal: a gentle, caring father and mother and the one child of each gender that tells us that this community has solved the population problem; the scenes of their warm, bantering conversations around the dinner table; their formal sharing (as required by the Rules) of feelings from their day and dreams from their night; the comfort and support they offer one another. But then we hear of "Birthmothers" and applications for children and spouses; we begin to wonder why there are no grandparents and to suspect what lies behind the parents' talk of "release."

Lowry has structured the intriguing details of this planned community with meticulous care, focusing particularly, through Jonas's eyes, on the education system that produces a society that functions by internalized values. At first it seems to be an autocratic state—an impression that is given credence by Orwellian images such as the rasping voices that chastise from ubiquitous speakers. But soon it is revealed that the community is ruled by an elected Committee of Elders and that the citizens long ago chose this controlled life. Each peer group of fifty children is called by their ages—Fives, Elevenses—and is distinguished by certain clothes, haircuts, and required behaviors that are appropriate for their stage of development. At eight they begin to spend their after-school hours volunteering in the various work of the community, and at twelve they are each given an appropriate "Assignment," based on the careful observation of the Committee of Elders, which will be their job for life.

When the fateful December ceremony comes, Jonas is stunned to learn that he has been appointed the new Receiver of Memory, the highest position in the community. Each day he goes to the rooms of the old Receiver of Memory, a reclusive elderly man whom he comes to call the Giver. There his innocence is gradually transformed as the old man transmits to him, often with great pain for Jonas, the memories of experiences and emotions that the people have chosen to banish from their minds so that they might sustain the illusion of social order and success. Jonas's first memory lesson is a sled ride that teaches him the concepts of cold and snow and of "downhill"—ideas that are new to him because the community has abolished weather and irregular terrain in the interest of efficiency. As the days wear on, Jonas experiences war and pain and love, and he begins to understand how his society has given up choice and freedom for control and predictability.

And then one day he asks to view a videotape of a "release" that his father has that morning performed on an unwanted baby at the community nursery and learns to his horror that the euphemism covers engineered death—for the old, for rule breakers, and for surplus or difficult infants. Watching his father sweetly wave bye-bye to the small corpse as it slides down the disposal chute, Jonas realizes with cold shock that his nurturing family is a sham, held together by trained reactions, not love, and that there is only hollowness at the heart of the society's life. He and the Giver hatch a plot to force the community to change: Jonas will flee, so that the memories he has assimilated will return to the people, forcing them to suffer and grow. But that night Jonas's father announces that Gabriel, the difficult toddler who has been temporarily sharing their home and whom Jonas loves, will be "released" the next morning. There is no time to carry out the plot; in the night, Jonas and Gabriel bicycle away.

And now we come to the inherent difficulty of every dystopian story—how to end. Basically, there are three possibilities: the protagonist escapes as the society collapses; the protagonist escapes with the intention of returning with the seeds of change; or the protagonist escapes, but it turns out to be an illusion. Lowry opts for elements of all three. Jonas journeys for days and, finally, at the end of his strength, comes to a place where there is snow, a hill, and a sled. Here the story, which up till now has been readable as an adventure tale, becomes symbolic and ambiguous as Jonas and the dying baby begin the sled ride toward the faint distant Christmas lights that are part of his memory of love. Is it a dream? Are they already dead? Or will they find a new life? Will the community they left behind reshape itself in a more human mold? Lowry refuses to provide a tidy ending. The challenge of the ambiguity is appropriate for the stature of this intricately constructed masterwork. As young adults seem to understand instinctively, it is not necessary to hold symbols up to the light of day to feel their underlying power in a well-told tale.

Monster as
Radical Change

EVERY DECADE OR SO a book comes along that epitomizes what has gone before and points the way to what is to come. In young adult literature, *The Catcher in the Rye* is such a milestone book, as are *The Outsiders* and *The Chocolate War*. And now Walter Dean Myers's stunning new novel, *Monster*, joins these landmark books. Looking backward, *Monster* is the peak achievement of a career that has paralleled the growth of the genre; looking forward, it is a perfect example of the revolutionary new literary direction Eliza Dresang describes in her recent critical study, *Radical Change: Books for Youth in a Digital Age*.

Dresang bases her theories on the idea that in our digital age, widespread exposure to electronic media, especially television, film, and computers, has changed the way we gather and process information, the patterns of our thinking. Young people, those she calls the "Net Generation," are particularly apt to be affected. Literature, and especially literature written for young people, is beginning to reflect this metamorphosis in ways Dresang terms "Radical Change." The indications of this in what Dresang refers to as the "handheld book" are seen in three main characteristics: connectivity, interactivity, and access. In other words, "RC" books

Originally published in "The Sand in the Oyster," *Horn Book* (November/December 1999): 769–73.

show "bits that are nonsequential and rearrangeable" that need to be linked in the reader's mind, rather than on the page, in order to make a linear pattern; they encourage readers to interact with the text and with one another by employing a variety of devices, among them ambiguity, and they break barriers for new formats, subjects, and voices. *Monster* fits this rather clinical list of symptoms, but also goes beyond, showing that this new thinking can free a master to create a work of great freshness and emotional and moral power.

Monster begins with a situation that will be familiar to readers of another quintessential RC book, Virginia Walter's *Making Up Megaboy*. As in that book, a store owner has been shot and killed; a boy is in jail awaiting trial. However, Myers's protagonist Steve Harmon, unlike Walter's enigmatic Robbie, speaks for himself and immediately engages our sympathies in his terror at the chilling behavior of the other inmates. In an innovative structure, the book uses two disparate forms of narration. Steve's fearful thoughts appear in handwriting on gray paper, and to make sense of the jail experience, he also begins to write a movie in his head—"a strange movie with no plot and no beginning." This film script, which appears in type on white paper, records the process of his trial, layered with flashbacks to the events leading up to the crime. Through "nonsequential and rearrangeable" thoughts, overheard remarks, and fragments of scenes, the story begins to emerge.

Steve at sixteen is a decent kid with two loving parents—he's interested in filmmaking, liked by his teacher—but with a reluctant but dangerous admiration for the tough guys on the street. A scene in which they ask him to be the lookout for a drugstore holdup ends without Steve's answer. He "looks away" in silence as the camera pulls back to show the bustling Harlem streets that have brought him to this temptation. Steve's role in the holdup is to check out the store beforehand and give the others a sign if there are police or other people inside. If all is safe, he is to do nothing. Does he accept the job? We know only that when the holdup took place, the store owner was shot and killed in a struggle over his own gun. As the trial proceeds, Steve silently cries out in the violence-haunted jail nights, "I didn't do nothing!" But to "do nothing" was his assignment, and *not* to "do nothing" is a tellingly double negative besides. "What did I do?" he thinks. "Anybody can walk into a drugstore and look around. Is that what I'm on trial for?" Notice the subtlety. Steve has not said he was there when the "getover" went down, but he has not said he was *not* there either.

Ambiguity, a quality Dresang feels is indicative of Radical Change, is inherent throughout *Monster* and provides opportunities for interaction, another RC marker, as we collect and weigh "evidence" for Steve's guilt or innocence in his own words, in the reactions and testimonies of the other characters, in the clues given by photographs and camera tricks. In another sense, this ambiguity also prompts interactivity between readers. Teachers will find it irresistible for passionate classroom discussions, and independent readers, teens and adults alike, will want to measure their interpretations against those of others. This was demonstrated recently in an interchange on the listserv CCBC-Net, sponsored by the Cooperative Children's Book Center of the University of Wisconsin at Madison. For almost a month, librarians and teachers made convincing but conflicting cases for various interpretations of Steve's part in the crime and the veracity of his narration and testimony. Like Pontius Pilate—and like Steve—they ended up by asking, "What is truth?"

Ginny Moore Kruse, the facilitator of that month's CCBC-Net discussion, made an end run around the question of Steve's guilt by focusing on his "struggle to maintain his sense of worth as a human being when he knows at least one person [the prosecuting attorney] has written him off with the term 'monster.' . . . In that person's view, Steve is already guilty. Why? Because he's black." Perhaps racism plays a part in Steve's case, but I would caution against ignoring the more universal implications of the desire to be seen as virtuous despite one's own or the world's assessment. "I want to feel like I'm a good person because I believe I am," Steve thinks, but at the same time he imagines the word *monster* tattooed on his forehead because "being in here with these guys makes it hard to think about yourself as being different." During the trial, his lawyer stresses over and over that the verdict depends on making Steve look good compared to the other "bad guy" defendants. The camera has the final word on this theme. After the verdict, Steve turns to embrace his attorney with outstretched arms, and when she rejects him the image grows grainy—"like one of the pictures they use for psychological testing, or some strange beast, a monster. The image freezes." Later, he agonizes, "What did she see?"—the last words of the novel.

Such integral use of cinematic techniques and other visuals breaks new ground for the young adult novel. The verbal narrative is enriched by quick cuts to scenes layered on top of one another, poignant close-ups of symbolic objects, split-screen montages, the opening and closing credit rolls, unexpected camera perspectives, even a cartoon interval. Although we are told that the script is being written by Steve as it happens, the movie is far beyond most sixteen-year-olds' capabilities in literary style and vocabulary, and eventually it takes on a life of its own by showing a private discussion between the judge and the attorneys, for example, or by commenting on the action outside of Steve's awareness. The inevitable question of whether *Monster* could be made into an actual film has to be answered in the negative. The shifts from faux-movie to interior narrative and the ambivalence between the two modes is what gives this indubitably literary work such high tension and interest for the perceptive reader. At first, the film script begins to seem like the only factual narration, the one dependable ground bass in this polyphony of voices, until Steve (and Myers) dispels that illusion by telling us, "I keep editing the movie, making scenes right. Sharpening the dialog. . . . The movie is more real in so many ways than the life I am leading." Again, what is truth?

Other uses of graphic elements are striking: the innovative half-jacket, a color photomontage wrapped around the black-and-gray reproduction of a fingerprint report printed on the cover, the word *monster* repeatedly scrawled across the script and then slashed out, or the page on which Steve writes *hate* many times "to make it look the way I feel." The photographs throughout go far beyond mere illustration to make their own points. In one set Steve is caught by the foggy lens of what seems to be a surveillance camera as he walks past shelves lined with merchandise. Captions ask, "What was I doing? What was I thinking?" Later, as the defense attorney presents Steve as a decent kid, these photos are echoed by another set which show him walking innocently on the street. Other photos are equally resonant in their references to mug shots, newspaper photos, television news, and other familiar media. So real are they in these references that one CCBC listserv member asked, "How can Steve, a fictional character, be photographed?" Behind the camera was the author's son, Christopher Myers, who won a Caldecott Honor in 1997 for his collaborative work with his father on *Harlem*.

A letter to the reader from Walter Dean Myers, which appeared only in the bound galley of the book, may shed some light on the author's intentions, if not the end result. In it he tells of the many inmates he interviewed at Greenhaven prison in upstate New York in search of answers to the question he posed himself, "What were the steps that led a person from innocence to criminal acts and, eventually, to prison?" He found that "there always seemed to be interim stages. Decisions to bend, not break, the law. . . . Each experience, basically involving a lack of a positive moral decision, would give permission for the next experience. Eventually a line would be crossed in which the probability of being caught was the only governing restriction."

Myers thinks that Steve is guilty ("*Monster* is the story of one young man, Steve Harmon, who has given himself the luxury of what seems to be a minor involvement in a crime"), but the book is perhaps richer than its author knows. Almost every sentence can be deconstructed for resonance, irony, multiple meanings; everything points to something else. In format and execution it is as au courant as the Internet, as modish as Radical Change. But the timeless theme of moral struggle emerges clear and multifaceted. At the heart of this complex intellectual and literary structure is a real boy whose suffering we come to identify with. *Monster*, like its predecessor *The Chocolate War*, raises questions it insists we must ask ourselves when we protest, "I didn't do nothing!"

The Last Cormier

THE PILE OF MANUSCRIPT PAGES LIES in the very center of my desk, neatly confined by a wide orange paper band. The title is barely showing, "The Rag and Bone Shop: A Novel by Robert Cormier." I sit and stare at the manuscript, reluctant to turn the page and end this moment of anticipation, of not-yet-knowing. Because this is the last time I—and the world—will read a new novel from Robert Cormier.

I remember all the other times of expectation and surprise—because a new novel from Bob was always a surprise. He had an almost superstitious fear of talking away a book, so I learned never to ask about a work in progress. But occasionally he would share a hint about the "what if"—the incident or idea that had triggered the story that was taking shape in his mind. So when a manuscript arrived and lay unopened on my desk, there would be a pause for delicious conjecture before I would turn the first page and discover a book that was unlike anything he had ever written before and at the same time completely *cormieresque* in its symbols and themes.

The first reading was for plot, simple abandonment to the pull of the good story. But the second reading was better—discovering the structure, the hidden meanings and secrets, the underlying

Originally published in "The Sand in the Oyster," *Horn Book* (September/October 2001): 623–26.

themes and shifts in voice that made his work so powerful. Then, after I had let my reactions jell for a few days, would come my favorite part, the phone call to discuss the new book with its author. What a privilege, what a joy! With characteristic modesty, Bob was always delighted to hear my praise, intrigued by my questions. He and I played with enigmas like whether Artkin was really Miro's father, whether Francis Cassavant was going to use that gun in his knapsack, whether Bob himself could "Fade."

But this time I'm all on my own. And it feels very lonesome as I turn that first page.

The Rag and Bone Shop. A puzzling title, even in context. Two years ago Bob had confided that he was working on a book he called "The Interrogator." "You mean like Brint?" I asked, thinking of Adam's sinister questioner in *I Am the Cheese.* "It *is* Brint," he said, enjoying my reaction. Later there was an interim title, "Down Where All the Ladders Start," drawn, like the final version, from the last stanza of a poem by William Butler Yeats, "The Circus Animal's Desertion."

I must lie down where all the ladders start,
In the foul rag-and-bone shop of the heart.

Appropriately enough, the couplet illustrates not only the state of mind of the soul-weary interrogator Trent (both protagonist and antagonist of the novel) but that of Cormier himself, in its insistence on the artist's painful need to commune with the dark places of the human heart. Cormier's last novel is utterly characteristic in this communication with darkness and in its themes of innocence corrupted, political authority misused, sin and confession and forgiveness and guilt, with an undergirding of religious faith and glimmers of hope just offstage. With the mastery of a literary lifetime in the rag-and-bone shop, Cormier lays out these themes, then turns them inside out, shows us their undersides, and leaves us with a handful of uneasy questions that we must answer ourselves.

The story centers on the long, excruciatingly intense interrogation of twelve-year-old murder suspect Jason by the cynical detective Trent. This tension-filled passage stretches taut over a third of the book, with a brief break—much needed by both the characters and the reader—during which Jason almost escapes but is cleverly thwarted by Trent. The first section of the book sets the stage for the interrogation. In the opening pages we see Trent at work extracting a confession of a hideous triple murder from a seventeen-year-old boy. The detective is cold, ambitious, fiercely devoted to his skill at questioning. "You are what you do," his wife had told him, "like an accusation," and he accepts the judgment willingly. Soon afterward we confront another hideous murder, as the body of seven-year-old Alicia is found battered in the woods.

But in-between is a typically *cormieresque* contrast, a lovely lyrical interlude in which Jason, a shy and sweet-natured seventh grader, wakes to contemplate the delicious freedom of the first day of summer vacation—a passage that turns ironic on a second reading, with our knowledge of what actually *does* happen on that day. On that afternoon, Jason goes, ostensibly, to visit a classmate, Brad, but his actual friend at that house is Brad's little sister Alicia, who amuses the lonely boy with her grandmotherly ways. Alicia is furious with her brother for some secret reason, so Brad soon leaves with his two buddies, and Jason is thus the last person to see the little girl alive—or "one of the last," as he desperately insists later.

When Alicia's murder is discovered, there are no clues, no evidence, no suspects. The police are under heavy political pressure from the media, the district attorney, even a senator, to find the killer, and so they send for Trent, a man who, it is rumored, "can get blood out of a stone." His assignment: a confession from Jason, the only suspect, because Alicia's brother has an alibi. The boy is brought to a waiting room in the police station, and he comes with innocent willingness because he wants to help, although he wonders "if coming here was a mistake." By the end of the waiting period that phrase has turned ominous, as he begins to sense his peril.

Trent carefully sets the stage—a small, cluttered room, hot and crowded, with two chairs of different heights—and the curtain goes up on the interrogation. The unequal contest has the horrid fascination of a weaving, hypnotic encounter between a cobra and a mouse, and its outcome is as inevitable. These chapters are thrilling in their intricate construction and elegance, the delicate perversity of their progression toward the unthinkable. Each one of Trent's questions changes the situation ever so slightly, moving Jason cleverly toward the confession the detective must have. At just the right moment, Trent shifts from opponent to advocate in a hideous parody of compassion. And with each question, Jason becomes more uneasy, blunders a bit further in the direction Trent has led, until suddenly the cage door clangs shut, and Jason realizes he is caught. His protests of innocence make it worse, as Trent points out with implacable illogic that his denial only proves his guilt.

In these brilliant passages, the point of view snaps back and forth, showing us the emotional thrust and parry of the two participants in a terrible game. Layered under the tension as the questioning proceeds is a second hidden conflict, when "in a blazing moment" Trent realizes that Jason is innocent but that his job is to get a confession nevertheless. Like a medieval torturer, his goal is not truth but an admission, and if the victim is destroyed in the process, that only confirms his guilt. Trent's twisted logic as he frantically tries to talk himself out of the impulse toward good parallels the twists that turn lies into truth. Jason desperately denies his guilt but finally begins to believe in it, to be tempted by the sweetness of forgiveness even without sin.

Questions of faith are inherent in the novels of the devoutly Catholic Robert Cormier, especially the nature of good and evil and their relationship to guilt and forgiveness. As always, he shows us the light by focusing on the shadow that is its consequence. In *The Rag and Bone Shop*, he has structured these ideas into the very shape of the narrative, comparing Trent's unholy work to that of a priest, but one who hears confessions to grant not absolution but indictment. The forgiveness he offers is an illusion, and the peace it brings is short-lived. Like a priest, he is weary with all the terrible deeds he has heard, "the unending litany of confessions," but he can find no peace for himself nor remission for his own sin of betrayal. When Jason emerges from the interrogation room he looks "broken, as if just lifted down from the cross." His ordeal leads not to redemption but further sin, as he desperately attempts to reconnect with reality by making his false confession true.

So once again we have a provocative and uncomfortable ending from Robert Cormier. But perhaps the key lies in the novel's two points of climax, two resolutions of tension, and in the second one we find that potential for goodness, that "if only" that always lies at the heart of Cormier's ethical statement. The first resolution comes with Jason's admission of guilt, a scene that, significantly enough, takes place offstage. The second, again seen indirectly, is the news of the true confession by the real killer. Suddenly everything is—or could have been—different. Trent could have felt a cleansing shame that might have led to his transformation. Jason could have felt released, vindicated, restored to life. But neither happens. Trent's conviction that "you are what you do" only gains dreadful resonance as he sees his career in ruins: *now I don't do anything.* Jason continues to be haunted and soiled by Trent's manipulations, trying with another murder to make sense of his disturbed universe.

And so as I come to the last sentence in the last book by Robert Cormier, I yearn to be able to pick up the phone, dial that familiar number, and ask for an easy answer, a neat and comfortable conclusion. But at the same time, I know that the answer would be "What do *you* think?" Because Robert Cormier in the humility of his greatness always hands it back to us.

Part Five

THE DAWN OF
GRAPHIC NOVELS

Maus: A Survivor's Tale

A HUNDRED YEARS FROM NOW, when the great-grandchildren of our teenagers flip on their computers to study the history of English literature, they will memorize the date 1986 as the year that marks the coming of age of the comic book. Last September a work was published that brought the potential of the form to dazzling fruition. That book is *Maus: A Survivor's Tale* by Art Spiegelman, an autobiographical "graphic novel" that tells the story of the suffering of the artist's father under Nazi persecution in Poland.

The comic strip has been around since before the turn of the century. Its long and steady development has built a foundation solid enough to allow constant exploration on the growing edge. There have been great comic strips, even some that have earned grudging admiration from the literary establishment (e. e. cummings's essay of tribute to Krazy Kat, for example). There have been great comic books, collections of episodes. There have been graphic novels of extravagant fantasy and satire. There have even been a few other realistic autobiographical graphic novels—most notably Harvey Pekar's splendid *American Splendor*. But until now there has been nothing that approaches the unity and coherence and the sustained narrative power of *Maus*. It is, in essence, the first of a new kind of literature.

Originally published in "The Young Adult Perplex," *Wilson Library Bulletin* (February 1987): 50–51.

But, in spite of the impressive reviews (and the Pulitzer Prize) that Spiegelman has earned, are teachers and librarians (not to mention publishers) ready to take the graphic novel seriously? The recent history of the form has estranged it from much of the reading public. During the sixties and seventies young cartoonists in their infatuation with the freshness of being able to say the unsayable and picture the unthinkable wallowed in imaginative violence and exuberantly detailed sex. The horrible and nauseating became de rigueur, and adult comics went underground in America. Now that the form has outgrown this adolescent need to shock, the pornographic aura still clings in the minds of many. Although early chapters of *Maus* were published in *Raw* magazine and although Spiegelman has here a subject for which the most detailed depiction of violence might be morally justified, his drawings have classic restraint. There is no gore, no close-ups of shootings and beatings, no screams of "Aieee!" The few scenes of mass carnage are seen from an emotional distance and have the silent rhythm of Greek friezes. In the forefront is the simple story of a very human man trying to survive with dignity in a world full of terror and menace in which he must hide in the walls like a rodent. The horror is pervasive and inherent, and the artist needs no cheap tricks.

The structure of *Maus* is intriguing. The first volume is subtitled *My Father Bleeds History*. (A second volume, *Maus: And Here My Troubles Began*, was published in 1991.) Artie, a cartoonist in his midthirties, goes to visit his aging father to talk to him about a project he has in mind, a comic book based on the old man's memories of the Holocaust. The father, Vladek Spiegelman, agrees to tell his story to his son, although he protests, "Better you should spend your time to make drawings what will bring you some money." As Vladek's tale proceeds chronologically, each episode is framed by a visit from Artie in which he struggles with his tortured relationship with his father. At the same time, the Holocaust story he is researching and plans to draw is the very story we are reading.

These three narrative levels intersect at several points with intricate reverberations. Artie shows his father the work in progress (which the reader has previously seen). "I've already started to sketch out some parts," he says. "I'll show you. See, here are the black market Jews they hanged in Sosnowiec" (an episode from the Holocaust story). "And, here's *you* saying, "Ach, when I think of them, it still makes me cry!" (an incident from the relationship story). And in the present Vladek looks at the picture of himself and says, "Ach, still it makes me cry." Add to this a fourth level, the fact that we know that this story is true, and it is likely that all three of these scenes really happened singly and together.

The structural centerpiece is entirely different in the emotional intensity of both style and subject—a short piece, first published in 1973, titled "Prisoner on the Hell Planet." It shows Artie's pain at the suicide of his mother, Anja, and it bursts off the page like a shriek of anguish. "This isn't like other comics—" says Mala, Artie's stepmother, who has happened on the piece in a magazine. "I tell you when Ruthie showed it to me I thought I'd *faint*, I was so shocked. It was so—so personal!" It is a relief to get back to the more universal emotions of the cool, meticulously detailed story of the tightening Nazi noose.

Spiegelman's mastery of structure is equaled by his skill at character. The portrait of his father is a rich, detailed likeness of a complex and contradictory personality. Vladek's actions and words reveal him. The drawings show only a rudimentary mouse face—a single line of pointed nose and two dots for eyes—with which the artist does manage nevertheless to convey some surprisingly subtle nuances of expression. The reader sees Vladek simultaneously as both an old and a young man, as he tells his story and as he appears in it. The elder Vladek is obsessive and miserly, a man who quarrels constantly with his second wife and who loves his son but shows it in paranoid, intrusive ways. He speaks with a clumsy accent. The young Vladek is elegant and articulate in his native Polish, a tender husband and father, a resourceful, quick thinker with an iron will to survive. The connection between the two is in the events that changed the one into the other.

As Vladek begins his story in 1935, we see him as a dapper young man courting Artie's mother, Anja, and marrying into her wealthy family. Soon after the birth of their first child, Richlieu,

Anja has a nervous breakdown, a first indication of the neuroti-
cism that would later lead to her suicide. Vladek accompanies her
to a luxury sanitarium, and on the way they see for the first time
Nazi flags in the villages. When they return home, the dark clouds
have begun to gather. Vladek is drafted into the Polish army and
captured by the Germans. As a prisoner of war he barely escapes
a mass execution of Jewish soldiers. Back home he is shocked to
discover that the Nazis have confiscated all the family's textile fac-
tories, and they are reduced to living on their savings.

The household numbers twelve: Anja's grandparents and father
and mother, her brothers and sisters and their children, Vladek
and Anja and their child, Richlieu. Gradually as the Nazis close in,
the number dwindles. Again and again what remains of the family
moves on, hiding in secret compartments in the coal cellar and in
the ceiling, foraging for food at night. At last they are betrayed and
taken to a depot to await transport to Auschwitz. Vladek bribes a
way out for himself and his wife but is unable to save her parents.
Vladek and Anja wander about, paying one person and then another
to conceal them, squeaking by in breathless hairbreadth escapes.
They get by on Vladek's hoarded money, on his wits and sheer force
of personality. When Anja wants to give up he exhorts her, "To die,
it's easy. . . . But you have to struggle for life!" At last they make
a desperate break for Hungary and are caught on the train. This
first volume of the story ends as they arrive at the dreadful gates
and are separated. "And we came here to the concentration camp
Auschwitz, and we knew that from here we will not come out any
more" says the old Vladek, staring into the past.

But the book is not over yet. Artie has been eagerly looking forward to reading his mother's version of these terrible events. Now
Vladek must confess that in a depression after her death he burned
all her notebooks and journals. The man who was so passionately
committed to saving this woman's life has now "killed" her for her
son by destroying her memories. Artie is bitterly angry, but he swal-
lows his rage and parts calmly with his father. In the last panel he
scuffs off, muttering darkly to himself, "Murderer!"

The matter of the animal metaphor in *Maus* bears some examination, both for its own interest and because naïve critics have found it trivializing to the subject. "Maus," of course, is German for "mouse." The Jews in Spiegelman's drawings are mice. Other nationalities also have animal identities: the Poles are pigs, the Germans cats, the Americans dogs. Yet this is no barnyard world like *Animal Farm*. Except for their pointed, whiskered faces, the characters are completely anthropomorphized. After a few pages we think of them as people, so much so that it is a surprise to glimpse a long tail under Anja's skirts or to see them don pig masks to go undetected among the Poles.

Spiegelman plays with these metaphors in literary ways, beginning with the pun in the subtitle. Obviously, the idea of cat-and-mouse games is appropriate in the way the Jews must hide by day in bunkers and tunnels and attics. Vladek has internalized this need; drawing a diagram of one of the family's bunkers, he tells Artie, "such things it's good to know exactly how was it—just in case." When Anja and Vladek crouch in one particularly damp cellar, she sees a scurrying shape and is terrified that it may be a rat. "They're just mice," Vladek comforts her. Less amusing is the opening quotation from Adolf Hitler: "The Jews are undoubtedly a race, but they are not human."

But what is the real function of these animal identities? There is a long literary tradition, going back before Aesop to the folktale, of masking our everyday human selves in story with the features of birds and beasts. This has been an especially common convention in the comic strip. Mice, beginning with Mickey and working down to Ignatz and Jerry, have long been leading actors for the cartoonist. When the drama is more serious, these animal tragedy masks have an elevating, distancing effect. Internal evidence for this point can be found in *Maus*. The characters in "Prisoner on the Hell Planet" are drawn as human beings, and the emotions are unbearably personal and intense. When the story comes back to Vladek's narrative and the Spiegelmans resume their mouse faces, the serene distance of classical pity and terror returns. The story becomes larger, more significant—less particular and more universal.

Maus has been analyzed and praised by some of the best critics in the business. To their voices this reviewer can add only one new thought: this is a book that is supremely important and appropriate for young adults. Not only because teenagers have always found the comic strip congenial, not only because it is a story of the pain of parent-child conflict, not only because it is a superbly original piece of literature, but also because it is a stunning evocation of the terror of the Holocaust—and we dare not let the new generation forget.

Whaam! in Paris

PARIS—Teenagers are not often conspicuous on the streets of the City of Light. Either they blend in or they are tucked safely away at home or at school. In any case, it is not until our second week here that we come across a bevy of YAs involved in a recognizable adolescent group activity. On the plaza of the Palais de Maillot, in the shadow of the Eiffel Tower, dozens of teenage hotshots are whirling on rollerblades to music that they alone can hear through their Walkman headphones. The next day we find another YA crowd underground at Pompidou Center. They have come there not to look at the modern art in the museum but to thumb through the modern art in the form of comic books in Whaam!—a basement bookstore.

Downstairs beneath an ordinary-looking souvenir poster shop, Whaam! is a treasure house for devotees of the *bande dessinee*, a French phrase that carries much more dignity than the English term, comic book. These volumes have sturdy bindings and are arranged in bins alphabetically by artist so that customers can go directly to their favorites. A sign taped to the wall gives notice that the latest issues of Gaston Lagaffe, Boule et Bill, Lieutenant Blueberry, Lucky Luke, Tintin, Alix, Asterix, and Achille Talon are on reserve at the desk.

Originally published in "The Young Adult Perplex," *Wilson Library Bulletin* (November 1982): 236–37.

On the first table, many of the books seem to be collections drawn from three magazines: *Pilote*, *(A Suivre)*—which means "to be continued"—and *L'echo des Savanes*. Flipping through *Pilote*, even without any knowledge of French, I am impressed with the range and variety of the stories and critical essays. A sophisticated soft-brushed and restrained pictorial version of De Maupassant stands next to an Achille Talon romp that ends with the Arc d'Triomphe being used as a wicket in the Grand Prix de Croquet. The stories in *L'echo des Savanes*, on the other hand, lean toward violent machismo. Both magazines pay tribute to American artists: *L'echo des Savanes* offers an edition of American comic art for ten francs, and *Pilote* includes drawings by Gahan Wilson and advertises a special Robert Crumb issue.

(A Suivre) is centered around a theme each month. An outstanding example was the John Lennon special done in 1981, still a big seller at Whaam! The leading comic strip artists of Europe were asked to take part in this memorial volume, and the list of the contributors is a checklist of who's who in *bande dessinee*. The stories are stunning in concert and execution. Comes illustrates a tale of night and snow in the stark style of a Japanese woodcut, with dizzying changes of perspective and scale; in it a Lennon figure finds a slant-eyed faerie and gives her a scarab to ride astride to the moon. Margerin offers a bitter satire on the commercial exploitation of "La Minute de Silence," and Boucq-Delan has a frumpy Eleanor Rigby wake Lennon from his coffin to lead him over the back wall of heaven to the Strawberry Fields. Druillet treats the theme with abstraction in an exploded geometric montage.

Browsing further, I find not only the luscious Barbarella, but her little sister Hypocrite, both the creations of Claude Forest. A less flamboyant heroine, drawn by Roger Leloup, is the Japanese teenager Yoko Tsuno, who uses her skill at electronics to triumph in episode after episode. Another gutsy young woman is the leading figure in *Les Passagers du Vent*, a five-volume historical adventure reminiscent of *Treasure Island* in period and setting.

Some of these comic books are actually comical. Le Genie des Alphages by F'Murr is a popular character, as is Andreacchio

Humberto's Mordillo. The latter strip resembles the style of the *Wizard of Id* and has appeared in the United States. (One set of panels spoofs French priorities: The little man is stranded on a desert island. A mermaid washes ashore. Overjoyed, he rushes into the bushes and returns with a frying pan.) I see some political satire, too, for instance, *Les Aventures de Madame Pompidou* by Cabu. And those feline favorites, Felix and Krazy, have always been beloved in France.

Stacked on one shelf are volumes and volumes of collections of vintage American comic series published by Futuropolis in French translation. They include not only the obvious choices (*Superman, Dick Tracy*), but other more obscure strips (*Jungle Jim, Polly and Her Pals, Mandrake the Magician*). The modern development of *bande dessinee* is also rooted in more traditional literary forms. The writings of H. P. Lovecraft are the subject of Alberto Breccia's suitably murky illustrations. Numa Sadoul and France Renonce have undertaken the ambitious task of rendering Wagner's *Ring of the Nibelung* in *bande dessinee*. The first volume—*L'Or du Rhin*—shimmers with the gleam of sunlight underwater and has the look of an archaic mural.

Classy, yes. But in America we have come to associate underground comics with sex and violence. Is that not an inseparable element of *bande dessinee* also? Over in a corner, behind the postcard rack, there is a section of frankly pornographic comics. Most of them are beautifully drawn creations of elaborate sadomasochistic fantasy. A specialized taste evidently, judging from the dust on the covers. But the pictures in many of the other books heaped on the tables in the center of the room are often sensual, sometimes sexually explicit, but not actually pornographic.

A troubling exception is the extremely interesting and innovative work of both Moebius and Philippe Druillet. In a typical Moebius strip, a man's female partner disintegrates in a bloody, orgasmic explosion. In *Vuzz*, by Druillet, a world is peopled with aliens in the shape of bursting phalluses. These artists are obviously two leading figures of *bande dessinee*. Many of their books are displayed, and a poster on the wall announces a major film with animation by

Moebius: *Les Maitres du Temps,* based on the novel *L'Orphelin de Perdide* by Stefan Wul. The sexual violence in their art seems to be antifeminist and often antihuman.

On the way out, I stop to chat with the proprietor. An older YA volunteers to translate for us. The proprietor tells me that there is an annual prize for best *bande dessinee* in France: it is given at a gathering of devotees in the town of Angouleme. Last year's winner was Cosey for *Jonathan, Le Berceau du Bodhisativa.* My translator tells me who he thinks are the very best in France. Moebius and Druillet, of course—and I am inclined to agree with him. Vive les YAs. They keep us from comfortable judgments.

Part Six

CENSORSHIP NEAR AND FAR

The Pottymouth Paradox

YESTERDAY I GOOGLED THE F-WORD. For a perfectly legitimate reason: I wanted some enlightenment on the growing paradox in YA lit of both a wider usage of and a narrower tolerance for obscenity. Searches on terms such as *profanity, censorship, obscenity,* even *bad words,* had been uninformative, and so I punched up the Big Daddy of swear words in English. A testament to the power of that word is the way the search made me feel paranoid and perverted—as if I might end up on a government list somewhere. After surviving the predictable onslaught of porn sites, I discovered a treasure: a long, thoughtful (but entertaining) academic article by Christopher M. Fairman for the Ohio State Moritz College of Law, examining the legal implications and the power of the word, drawing on the research of etymologists, linguists, lexicographers, psychoanalysts, and social scientists. Among other fascinating data, he reveals that the earliest citations of the word go back to the fifteenth century, and even then the word appears encoded, in the way that contemporary writers less foolhardy than Fairman resort to *f--k.* The title of the piece, of course, is *Fuck.*

In this column, let us use the word as a marker for the pitifully sparse vocabulary of obscenity and profanity in written English, although the growing numbers of standard-bearers for word purity

Originally published in "The Sand in the Oyster," *Horn Book* (May/June 2007): 311–15.

can even raise objections to proper names for body parts, like *scrotum*, as demonstrated by the brouhaha over this year's Newbery winner. And certainly censorship is a much more complex dilemma than just reactions to "bad language."

However, Fairman goes straight to the root of the problem as it is acted out in many a censorship battle over young adult literature: "*Fuck* is a taboo word. The taboo is so strong that it compels many to engage in self-censorship. This process of silence then enables small segments of the population to manipulate our rights under the guise of reflecting a greater community"[1] And yet despite the ever-increasing vigilance of these "small segments of the population," the language in some YA novels gets raunchier and raunchier. Take just one example from last year's crop, *Nick & Norah's Infinite Playlist*, by Rachel Cohn and David Levithan. In the book's first two chapters alone, the word *fuck* appears twenty-two times, other obscenities twenty-five times. And that's not unusual, as any reader of YA novels will testify. Of course, in this story about the inner workings of the punk-rock music scene, as in other novels about war or urban poverty or deeply troubled teens, such language is completely appropriate for veracity and accurately reflects the characters' speech.

At the same time that such YA novels are being accepted with hardly a blink, a single *damn* can be enough to disqualify a title for school or book club purchase. Why is this part of the YA market so much more sensitive to spicy language? According to Shannon Maughan in a recent *Publishers Weekly* article:

> School library materials traditionally come under more scrutiny than those at public libraries, for a variety of reasons. School librarians are usually working within a smaller budget than their public library counterparts and have an additional duty to support the school's curriculum as well as answer to school administrators. This frequently means tighter guidelines for purchasing fiction. In addition, because students in a school setting are a more "captive" audience than patrons of a public library, the materials that students have access to at school are usually more closely monitored by parents.

Well aware of these factors, many school librarians and teachers are more vigilant than ever about selecting materials that will
not raise parental or community concern. Unfortunately, such
vigilance can lead to self-censorship that keeps books from getting onto, or remaining on, school library shelves.[2]

Publishers, of course, are well aware of which of their books
should be tidied up for possible school purchase. I have heard several stories recently from YA authors who have agreed to requests
from their editors to change one or two words in a book so that it
would qualify for acceptance in these less tolerant but lucrative
markets. Sometimes this request comes from the book club or book
fair managers. Occasionally only the library edition is expurgated,
and the trade copy retains the offensive word (collectors take note).
Or if the deal is negotiated after the book has been published, the
book fair may take on the paperback rights and reprint the cleaned-
up book themselves.

During a recent visit to the Kerlan Collection of Children's
Literature at the University of Minnesota ("Researching YA Lit in
the Elysian Fields"), I found evidence of many editorial discussions
with authors about obscenities. A consistent theme was the editor's
apologetic embarrassment about asking for language revisions. In
the Kerlan files I found a letter from Atheneum editor Ginee Seo
to author Chris Lynch about his 2005 novel *Inexcusable* that vividly
illustrates just how difficult this area is for editors who are committed to free expression:

> And—take a deep breath here—I cleaned up the language. This
> was a really difficult thing to do, as I think you can understand.
> Believe me, I agonized over this. I don't, as a rule, like to do this
> on young adult books. I don't want to compromise on how kids re-
> ally talk. I don't want to acknowledge those fucking gatekeepers.
> But in this case, Chris, I feel the book is so important—the mes-
> sage it's sending to young men so crucial—that I feel very strongly
> that this is a book that can and should be used in schools, and
> therefore I want to give it every advantage. You will say, okay,
> but won't some schools turn away from the book because of the

subject matter anyway? Yes, some of them will. But other schools won't—and I don't want to make the argument for using the book that much harder for the teachers who decide to take it on. And if that means taking out a few fucks and shits from the narrative, I can live with that—and hope you can, too. Well, think about it, anyway.[3]

Recently, Elizabeth Bicknell, editorial director of Candlewick Press, talked with me about her similar difficulties in striving for written speech that accurately reflects the characters without limiting the book's availability. Most spectacular was the edit on Adam Rapp's *Snowfish* 33. Originally, she says, "the language was a lot stronger"—a possibility readers of this gritty novel will find hard to imagine. Bicknell toned the wording down to where she herself felt comfortable with it. Interestingly, it was not the big F and its variants but more colorful slang that she found disquieting. Rapp had said that releasing profanity allowed him to release the truth, but he and Bicknell found that when the profanity was later removed, the truth remained.

Bicknell also revealed that when Ron Koertge's *Brimstone Journals* was accepted by the Junior Literary Guild in 2001, it was the first time that august body had ever sponsored a book with *fuck* in its pages. Later, Koertge, perhaps made cautious by this near squeak, took all the "bad language" out of his spring 2007 novel *Strays,* then put it back when Bicknell felt that the sanitized book had lost its punch. Just this year, editor Deborah Noyes's fall 2007 short-story collection *The Restless Dead* was nixed by the Guild until one *fucking* was removed. But through all these negotiations, Bicknell asserts one overriding principle: "It's always the author's choice."

Books that have no expectation of school or book club purchase can, and do, reach out freely to all the unlimited possibilities of the English language as it is spoken in many different places and situations. When the forces of "language purity" come across such books, they wallow in their outrage and strategize how to keep them away from readers. A spectacular example is PABBIS (Parents

Against Bad Books in Schools), whose website, www.pabbis.com, reproduces the naughty bits in young adult books, sometimes pages and pages from a single novel, so that heavy-breathing would-be censors can read all the dirty parts without the bother of reading the book, and then follow the website's instructions on how to get the book banned.

We seem to have a dichotomy developing here. On the one hand are the "fuck-free" books with potential for book clubs and school libraries and on the other are the "chock-full-o'-fuck" books accepted by bookstores and public libraries. Quality is not a related factor; award books can come from either sector. Perhaps, if we are careful to be clear about its shape, this dichotomy is not a bad thing. Freedom of expression is readily available to authors, and those buyers who prefer books without swear words can have their books, too.

NOTES

1. http://law.bepress.com/cgi/viewcontent.cgi?article=5152&context =expresso (accessed March 2, 2007).

2. http://www.publishersweekly.com/article/CA6416737/html (accessed March 2, 2007).

3. Letter from Ginee Seo to Chris Lynch. Reprinted with permission from the author.

Who's Afraid of the
Big Bad . . . ?

A FEW MONTHS AGO there was an impassioned discussion on the listserv childlit about a note that was sent home from school to alert parents that the movie *Schindler's List* would be shown in class but assuring them that the sexual references would be edited out. What peculiar priorities and attitudes this reflects! Exposure to sex is perceived as more disturbing to young people than exposure to the greatest horror of the twentieth century. Could there be a clearer statement of the sex negativity of our society?

Since trying to sort out the confused nature of YA publishing toward the f-word and other verbal obscenities in fiction for teens ("The Pottymouth Paradox"), I have found myself wondering why the very mention of sex in YA novels arouses such wrath and indignation in certain folks. The Office for Intellectual Freedom of the American Library Association has documented that the top reason for challenging library material is "sexually explicit" content (although they also point out that "books are challenged with the best intentions—to protect others, frequently children, from difficult ideas and information")

But surely it is apparent that while sex may involve "difficult ideas and information," it is an overriding interest with teens, and they need to know not only the facts, but the feelings and pitfalls

---

Originally published in *Horn Book* (September/October 2007): 683–87.

of human coupling. Why, then, do so many of us feel uneasy about giving them the knowledge of how sexuality works, or doesn't work, in the world?

When my own four children were teens, my sex education method was to leave selected YA books lying around for them to pick up if they wished. Sometimes they didn't, but I was savvy enough to know that one's own mother is the last person in the world with whom one wants to chat about sex, even if she is writing a book on teen sex education manuals—which I was at the time. So I persisted with the literary method, and when my boys were old enough to date I let them bring their girlfriends home with them, provided they availed themselves of the bowl of condoms I kept on the bathroom sink.

Of course, that was a different time—pre-AIDS and barely post-hippie. But as a product of that era, I find it very difficult to understand parents who go ballistic at the unzipping of a fly in teen fiction. So I set out to do some research by talking with not only a psychiatrist and a psychological family counselor, but with a variety of Concerned Parents, who shall all remain anonymous.

"What are your feelings about sexual references and scenes in fiction for teens?" I ask them. The psychiatrist surprises me. "I know I'm conservative about this," he says (I hadn't noticed him being conservative about anything else), "but I don't think young teens should read this stuff." Then he explains his theories about the developmental tasks of various ages—ending with "about the age of ten to fifteen, learning to get along with peers, and fifteen up, learning how you fit into the world. If you discover the easy pleasures of sex too early, there is a danger that you'll get fixated at that point and never work through the other learning stages. Besides, the writers just throw in these scenes to be titillating and sell books."

"Whoa!" I cry, stung. "I know these writers, and I know that's not true. Most of them are just trying to tell kids the truth about sex and love."

"Weeellll," he muses. "If it's about love, I guess that's okay. It's just the separation of the two that bothers me."

The psychological family counselor comes up with a different reaction. She feels it is all about fear—fear of loss of parental control, fear of your own children showing sexual interest and becoming sexual beings. But why are books the particular target? A friend had suggested that books are somehow seen as sacred, a medium that should be pure and "enlightening"—a term that pops up often in censorship hearings. But the counselor is more pragmatic: "Books are the target because their availability can be influenced," she guesses. "Movies and television are owned by big corporations and are unreachable, but the school board and the library trustees are right there for protests, and the local newspaper loves it. Offended parents feel they can make a difference on that level, and they're right."

The conversations with Concerned Parents generate more heat. "It's undermining parental authority," says one CP emphatically. "There are many definitions of responsible sexual conduct—for instance, Muslim parents might be offended even by descriptions of flirtatious glances between a boy and a girl. I want to teach my kids my own values. Authors have a very real responsibility not to guide kids into behaviors and attitudes that are going to be bad for them."

And here I catch a glimpse of the unspoken assumption that underlies the whole structure of protest. "Do you believe then, that any depiction of sex is a model for the behavior of the reader and will be acted upon?"

"Certainly," she asserts. "What they read is what they're going to do. You're learning from your reading, always. It's even been scientifically proven that viewing or reading about violence leads to violent actions, so it's probably the same with sex."

This puts me in a tight corner. How can I claim that my beloved YA literature has no effect on teen behavior? While I'm trying to think of how to change the direction of the conversation, she points out, "Besides, books read at school have a certain authority." I have to agree with her on that. There is an ascending scale of implied authority and thus parental sensitivity from a book shelved in the public library, a book shelved in the school library, a book on a read-

ing list, and a book assigned for class discussion. "Yes, I agree that
you have a right to limit your own child's reading. But does that give
you the right to limit every child's reading?"

"Absolutely. Shouldn't we all look out for each other?" She folds
her arms, and I refrain from reminding her that two minutes earlier
she had said that there are many definitions of responsible sexual
conduct.

Another CP reflects the widespread underlying notion that
liberals have a hidden agenda for promoting sexy books in schools.
She whips out a computer printout. "Look here," she says. "This
tells what's behind all this filth in books." I see that the clipping is
a news article quoting the website PABBIS (Parents Against Bad
Books in Schools).

> The un-American ALA has taken the American constitutional
> right of freedom of speech and has perverted it into their right
> to push graphic and explicit smut on children. ALA and ALA
> affiliate brown boot bullies are constantly working to implement
> their weird social Marxist agenda. What started, purportedly, as
> a professional union-like organization for librarians has morphed
> into a powerful, dangerous, leftist, extremist organization. The
> ALA believes "anything goes at any age" and that there is no
> difference between children and adults. ALA and ALA affiliates
> decide what books your children should read. They push smut
> in both public and school libraries. They decide what is read in
> English class. Their vision of what is best for your child doesn't
> include traditional classic literature. Smut-filled, "culturally di-
> verse," easy-reading books are being pushed instead[2].

After I get my breath back I go home and surf the net for PAB-
BIS (www.pabbis.com), Facts on Fiction (www.factsonfiction.org),
Citizens for Literary Standards in Schools (www.classkc.org), and
other websites who take it as their mission to point out or print every single word of the naughty bits in children's and YA lit and teach
horrified parents how to take action to get such books banned.
Reading through their statements of purpose and their reports on

action, I see the same familiar unexamined assumptions: that any mention of sex is by definition bad; that depiction results in behavior, even when that behavior is clearly shown to be undesirable; that their own teachings of values are easily wiped out by a passage in a book; that an evil "them" wants to corrupt their children.

In addition, I find evidence of a massive lack of literary sophistication. When interpretation depends on irony, metaphor, allegory, figurative language, or any kind of subtlety in characterization, these folks simply don't get it. The Facts on Fiction site, which rates hundreds of classroom standards on a complex system of possible offenses, marks Dickens's *A Christmas Carol* down for "bad attitude" of a character, presumably Scrooge.[3] And in scoring C. S. Lewis's great Christian allegory, *The Lion, the Witch, and the Wardrobe*, there are negative marks for witchcraft but no acknowledgement of the book's religious content[4].

And over all of these websites hangs the bad smell of sexual obsession, the inevitable partner of sex negativity. Classic works of YA literature become unrecognizable lists of "dirty" words and "smutty" scenes totally without context except to set up the sexual action. There is something truly nasty here, and it isn't the YA novels from which these words and scenes are wrenched. PABBIS is especially lascivious as it drools over the precise scoring of "vividness/graphicness" in descriptions of forbidden subjects. Here, for example, is their scale on "description of breasts," in their own words:

Basic: large breasts
Graphic: Large, voluptuous bouncing breasts
Very graphic: large, voluptuous bouncing breasts with hard nipples
Extremely graphic: large, voluptuous bouncing breasts with hard
    nipples covered with glistening sweat and bite marks[5]

I await the day with trepidation when kids discover that they can read all the "good parts" of YA novels online without bothering to turn the pages of a book. When that time comes, who's going to censor the censors?

Notes

1. www.ala.org/ala/oif/bannedbooksweek/challengedbanned/challenged banned.htm (accessed June 5, 2007).

2. Ray Strohm. "X-rated 'children's' books outrage students' parents." World Net Daily, March 15, 2006, http://www.prisonplanet.com/articles/march2006/150306_b_X-rated.htm (accessed June 12, 2007).

3. http://factsonfiction.org/content/review_details.aspx?isbn=9780553212440subject=7 (accessed June 9, 2007).

4. http://factsonfiction.org/content/review_details.aspx?isbn=0064409422&subject=1 (accessed June 9, 2007).

5. http://www.pabbis.com/bookreview.html (accessed June 7, 2007).

Perplexing Censorship
in Germany

BONN, WEST GERMANY—An official government agency for censoring books for youth? Shades of *Fahrenheit 451!* Last year in Munich when I first heard of the existence of the Bundesprufstelle fur jugendgefahrende Schriften, I was intrigued. How could such a bureau function in a democracy that is ostensibly committed to free speech? Our itinerary led south that year, and my curiosity was never satisfied. Now this year we are back in Northern Europe, and I have fumbled my way through the bureaucracy to make an appointment with the Bundesprufstelle. The bureau head, Rudolf Stefen, is away on holiday, but the second-in-command, Elke Monssen-Engbeding, will be glad to talk to me.

On the doorstep of the agency, upstairs in a very pleasant and unbureaucratic-looking shopping mall, I decide to concentrate my questions on matters of function and let the ethics of censorship fall where they may. After all, we know that free access for youth is the only right position, I think smugly as I go up the steps. In less than five minutes my convictions are to be badly shaken.

In their modern, book-lined offices I am welcomed cordially by Monssen-Engbeding and two of her colleagues, jurists Waltraud Diop and Christine Bolchenberg. They have decided to pool their

Originally published in "The Young Adult Perplex," *Wilson Library Bulletin* (October 1984): 130–31.

knowledge of English for the interview, and they giggle a bit about it. Far from the dour repressive types I had expected, these young women are cheerful and matter-of-fact. As I entered the office they clicked off a television monitor. "Much of our work right now is with videos," they explained. By this they meant videotapes made for home viewing. Television broadcasting in Germany is government originated and has its own set of standards.

Coffee is served, and we begin by putting our heads together— with the help of a dictionary—to work out an acceptable translation of the name of the bureau. They are part of the Ministry of Health and Youth, and Bundesprufstelle fur jugendgefahrende Schriften translates into English as "Federal Authority for Evaluating Books (or Writings) Dangerous to Youth." They are insistent on the term "dangerous." "'Problem books?' No, that is too soft. Here, we show you." And they turn on the monitor. "This video is called 'Eaten Alive.'" We settle back to watch.

From the first frame the screen is filled with images ghastly beyond lunacy. A pile of gnawed, blood-clotted human limbs in the grass, crowned with a staring, severed head. A few feet further on, a wild-eyed woman tearing with bloody mouth at a handful of dangling intestines. A group of people standing over a naked young woman spread-eagled on the ground. A man raises a long knife to the sky, then bends over and seizes her breast, the knife descends, the camera moves in for a close-up. "Stop!" I implore, cringing. "Turn it off, please!" They smile a bit at my reaction and put in another tape. "This one was made in America. It's called 'Mother's Day.'" Again not one second is wasted: a man slams a machete through the closed window of a car to decapitate the driver; the head falls forward and blood spurts up from the veins. He drags a girl from the other seat, slams her onto the hood of the car, unzips his fly to rape her while a second man batters her with his fists. Screams, blood, smashed teeth. An older woman appears and commands them to stop. "That is Mother," Diop explains. "They are her sons and they must bring young women to Mother because she loves to kill." The bloody victim begs for mercy and so do I. "Please, that's enough. I'm sorry, but I can't watch this. How can you look at it all day long?"

They shrug. "So you see why we say this is dangerous to youth."

"Dangerous to youth! I'd say these things are dangerous to everybody!" I hear myself say.

"Yes, but in Germany it is forbidden to control media, the press," they admonish. "Adults must be able to decide for themselves if they want to look at this."

Thus chastened, I listen sympathetically as they explain the workings of their organization. The BPS has jurisdiction only over the reading and viewing of young Germans under the age of eighteen. They do not have power to judge all published materials, only those books, magazines, newspapers, and videos referred to them for examination by local youth welfare agencies: the Bundesprufstelle itself cannot initiate a hearing. The actual evaluation is done by a board of twelve people meeting once a month in Bonn. The shifting membership of this board is drawn from a pool of seventy-two experts from eight different areas: art, literature, booksellers, publishers, youth organizations, youth welfare boards, teachers, and the clergy. In addition, the pool includes twenty-seven representatives from the "Lande," or local states. The experts are appointed for a three-year term by their own organizations, such as the Teachers' Guild, and they are paid only their travel expenses. But where are librarians represented here? The term "booksellers" also includes librarians, they explain, and in addition, a number of the representatives from the Lande are heads of libraries.

When a hearing is held, the publisher first presents a defense. Then he leaves the room, and the board reaches their decision. Eight votes are required for a judgment. In about twenty percent of the cases, they decide the video or book is not dangerous. Publishers may appeal to the courts on grounds of faulty procedures but not for the decision itself. Once a book or video is forbidden, or "indexed" ("'Forbidden' is not the right word," my hosts said. "Because for adults, you see, it is not forbidden."), it is listed in an official publication called the BPS Report. Video shops, bookstores, and libraries may subscribe at a small charge, although subscriptions are not obligatory.

How is the law enforced? In the case of videos, an indexed tape may not be sold to anyone under eighteen nor displayed where they might see it. Advertising, too, is restricted to rooms for adults only. The same rule applies to books in libraries and bookshops: the indexed titles cannot be displayed, sold, or loaned to young people. Enforcement is up to local police; they make unannounced inspections from time to time to make sure that indexed items are not on display. ("It is the duty of the police to control the shops because there is a law.") If they find a violation, the matter goes to court, and the penalty is a fine (or prison) based on the daily income of the defendant.

The image of a policeman strolling in to check the shelves and then hauling the head of acquisitions off to court is a particularly chilling one for American librarians. How does this affect library collection policies? A local constable would probably only point out the shelving error if he found an indexed book in the open stacks, admitted the three jurists. They had never heard of a case in which a library was fined. However, indexing has a chilling effect on purchase. The bookseller informs libraries when a book on order is indexed, and then "they send it back to the publisher," fearing that owning a forbidden book might cause them to inadvertently break the law if it wandered onto the wrong shelf.

For the same reasons serious bookstores are reluctant to purchase indexed material. This exerts financial pressure on publishers of indexed books, although the effect on videos is not so clear. The BPS can bring additional pressure to bear in the case of books in series or magazines. If three individual issues in a year are indexed, then the BPS has the option of indexing the entire magazine or series for one year unless the publisher agrees to clean up its content. As an example, the jurists show a copy of "Exquisit Bucher," a pornography series by a large Munich publisher. I also notice in the BPS Report that *Hustler* magazine has been proscribed until January 1985. *Bravo*, the most popular teen magazine in Europe has several times been under fire for articles endorsing drug use.

The criteria for judging materials are laid down quite specifically in the law. Violations fall into seven categories. *Gewalttatig-
keit*, or excessive violence, is the most common offense of videos
that I had seen. *Pornographie* was also no surprise. *Drogenkonsum*
refers to the promotion of drug abuse. *Frauendiskriminierung* is the
depiction of women as "things to buy." Most interesting politically
are the remaining three categories: *Rassenhass*, *NS-Ideologie*, and
Kriegsverherrlichung—racial hatred, Nazi ideology, and the glorification of war. Such books are available in Germany but only outside
the regular commercial bookselling channels, the jurists clarified,
from "special" publishers who sell only by mail order.

Certain considerations override the seven deadly sins listed
above. The most obvious, of course, is literary quality. Is it art or
pornography? is the question most frequently debated by the board.
Fanny Hill, for example, is available to young people, as are the
works of Henry Miller and the Marquis de Sade. Historical importance, too, can justify a work. *Mein Kampf* is not indexed. If a book
is out of print and only available in a limited number of copies,
the board might not bother indexing it. And they cannot consider
political books, with the exception of the three categories of racial
hatred, Nazism, and glorification of war. Judgments in these areas
can be complex. For instance, a collection of pages from *Der Adler*,
a Nazi magazine originally disseminated during World War II, was
subject to indexing because the collection was published in 1977,
although copies of the magazine itself are not restricted.

Do they attempt to differentiate between what is appropriate
for young children and what is appropriate for teens? No, that
would be too confusing, they answer. Do they ever judge children's
or young adult books? No again; they are only protecting young
people from harmful books written for adults.

What was the most controversial BPS case? "Oh, Harold Rob-
bins," they remember, chuckling. "A book called *Goodbye, Janette*.
Many loud people objected." But the judgment stood nevertheless.
Later, glancing through the BPS Report for other familiar names, I
see that 513 videos and 298 books have been indexed. ("The work

of four years," they said.) Most are plainly hard-core pornography. There are a number of comics, particularly the works of Georges Pichard, U-Comix, and the American In-and-Out Comics. The venerable *Marijuana Growers' Guide* from And/Or Press in Berkeley is listed along with other drug titles, and *The Story of O* in a number of editions. There are some books of Nazi propaganda. Among the videos, Bruce Lee is the most frequent offender, and cannibalism seems to be a popular theme.

As I am leaving, the jurists ask a parting question. "How are these things handled in America?" I am at a loss to sum it up in a few sentences. "Well, with us," I falter, "it is not so clear. It can be very confusing. Not all in order as it is with you."

Visiting Dubrovnik Public

DUBROVNIK—the city George Bernard Shaw called "the pearl of the Adriatic, a paradise on earth"—is very beautiful with its massive city walls and red tile roofs surrounded by a turquoise sea. In this city, built in the fifteenth century, it is not surprising to find a library in an ancient monastery. What is surprising, and what is characteristic of Yugoslavia, is the casual blend of the very old with the very modern. The library occupies the top floor, over a smart patio restaurant and a cinema. Upstairs the high windows filter the brilliant sunlight over a pleasant room with comfortable upholstered reading chairs and well-filled shelves.

I am talking with Ingrid Pavlicevic and Ksenija Brobora, librarians at the main branch of Dubrovnik Public, or Popular Library. Ingrid, dark-haired and young, is the chief, and blonde, Slavic-looking Ksenija is a librarian. Both women are dedicated book people.

First, we get the statistics out of the way. There are two branches plus the main library, and the system is affiliated with the Scientific Library. The main library has 40,000 volumes, most of them in Serbo-Croatian, but also in Slovenian and all the other languages of Yugoslavia. There are some gift books in the major European languages: English, French, Italian, German (I notice

Originally published in "The Young Adult Perplex," *Wilson Library Bulletin* (November 1983): 212–13.

the omission of Russian). The library is not a new thing, Ingrid and Ksenija hasten to explain. Dubrovnik has had a public library for forty years but only in the last six years has it been housed in these modern quarters. Users may borrow three books for fifteen days, and children qualify for a library card as soon as they enter elementary school. The fee is 150 dinars a year, which translates to only $1.50—we have been told by several people that the average skilled worker earns about $130 to $150 a month.

Librarians may be trained on two levels: university and secondary grammar school. System-wide, there are seven "high librarians," or university-trained librarians, and nine of the second category, which seems like a large staff for three libraries until I notice the lack of clerical workers. Tourists and other foreigners may use the reading room, but may not borrow books because "they are here for only one to two days, and then . . . " Ksenija shrugs expressively.

We talk about funding, and as usual I am almost immediately lost in the labyrinth of the Yugoslavian political system. The agency is S.A.Z. (roughly translated as Independent Community for Culture), and it seems to be part of the municipality. What is clear is that S.A.Z. distributes the money for all kinds of cultural activities according to demonstrated need. The library must submit a "works plan" every six months to show its circulation, membership, books cataloged, and so forth, in order to guarantee continued funding. Do they feel libraries get a fair share of the money? "Ah, no," they lament, "the library comes always at the tail."

How much world literature has been translated into Serbo-Croatian, I wonder. Everything, they assure me, and bring out a copy of *E.T.: The Extraterrestrial* to prove the point. Their patrons are well acquainted with foreign literature and sometimes even prefer to read in the original language. "You know our Nobel Prize writer, Ivo Andric? *The Bridge on the River Drini?*" asks Ingrid. Sheepishly, I admit I don't. "And poetry," adds Ksenija. "Our people like poetry very much, especially love poems. There are many modern Yugoslav poets and they are very popular. We are a musical people." As a lifelong fan of the music and dance of this country, I don't need to be convinced of that.

Ingrid brings coffee, and we get to the subject of teenagers.
Because it is an educational center, Dubrovnik has many young
people. Children from the farms and villages are sent to live and go
to school here when they are eight years old. The Economics University, Touristic School, and Music School draw older teenagers.
So a good part of the library's work is with this age. Ksenija outlines
a familiar problem: "It is very difficult to find a good book for them
because they grow up quickly and they think what you give them is
a children's book. What they want is a woman's love story, like you
buy everywhere in the kiosks."

"In America we have special books written just for teens,"
I begin. But they nod impatiently and bring me one in Serbo-
Croatian—*Gininazijalka* by Anton Ingolic, with a rock group and
a pretty YA on the cover. The German author Hedwig Courths-
Mahler is the most popular, but naturally none of her books are
on the shelf right now. "Love stories with happy endings," disdains
Ingrid. "It is better when they read Thomas Hardy."

"Ah, yes, love stories with sad endings," I tease. Boys have different tastes, they explain. Boys like war stories, science fiction,
authors like Jack London, Zane Grey, Jules Verne, Robert Louis
Stevenson, Harriet Beecher Stowe ("*Uncle Tom's Cabin?*" I ask incredulously. Yes.) "A few girls read these books, but it is harder for
them." A very popular book just now is *Christiane F.*, the German
story about teenage drugs and prostitution. "Our young people have
none of these drug problems, you understand, but they are curious
to know about these things."

Here is the opening I have been looking for. "In America this
book is sometimes considered very controversial, and librarians may
have difficulties if a parent objects to it. What would you do if there
was a protest?" They seem to be puzzled by my question. "Well,
but we make the selection, and that is it." Ksenija tries to carry
it further by explaining that she would dissuade a young person
from borrowing a book that was too mature. "Anyway, we have not
experienced that kind of problem." Sex education is not especially
interesting to teenagers, because they study it at an early age and

they already know it all. And "erotics" she shelves way up high. Ksenija demonstrates.

I push further. "Are you saying that you two do all the book selection, and nobody tells you what you may buy?" Of course, they insist. The National Library sends them guidelines of what proportion of the collection should be fiction, belles lettres, and so on, but these are for assistance, not as rules. "As you see here, we even have books by a writer like Leon Uris, and he is an anti-Communist author."

What would they do about an anti-Tito book? "Well, of course, such a book would not be written." (I almost believe them. We have seen convincing evidence everywhere of the people's love for their late leader.) "And if it was written somewhere else, it would not be translated. So it would not be a problem," they answer cheerfully.

Ingrid adds an afterthought. "Our National Library tells us when certain books are not good for libraries to have, and, of course, then we don't buy them." But then they confer and remember a book that had some anti-Tito sentiments. If they had bought that book, they would have kept it in a special place. And if someone had a good reason to read it—a journalist who was doing a piece for a newspaper, for instance—that person would be given the book if he asked for it. "Ah," I say. "We call it limited access." They nod happily, and Tito's picture beams benignly down on us from its place on the wall.

Part Seven

INSIDE ALA

The Not-So-Smart Alex

AMID ALL THE CRIES OF ACCLAIM for the American Library Association's new Alex Award, I find myself a dissenting voice. The effort to honor the year's ten best adult books for teenagers leaves me profoundly uncomfortable. The first award list, chosen by a committee of ALA's Young Adult Library Services Association and sponsored by the Margaret Edwards Trust, was introduced in June at the annual conference this year with great hoopla. Now that the huzzahs have died away, I am left with the conviction that such a move "to help librarians encourage young adults ages twelve to eighteen to read by introducing them to high quality books written for adults" (as the official statement has it) is regressive.

It is appropriate that this award is named for the patron saint of YA librarianship, Margaret Alexander Edwards, whose intimate associates called her Alex. Edwards's pioneering work at Enoch Pratt Free Library in Baltimore during the 1940s and 1950s set the model and standards for the specialty, and—as her book *The Fair Garden and the Swarm of Beasts* clearly reveals—she built her YA services around carefully chosen adult books. She and her staff combed the stacks for such cheerful goodies as *Cheaper by the Dozen* and *Mrs. Mike* and promoted them energetically to their young patrons.

Originally published in "The Sand in the Oyster," *Horn Book* (September/October 1998): 632–35.

But what we forget is that Margaret Edwards had to work so
hard to find adult reading that interested teens precisely because
there was very little young adult literature available to them: the
term itself did not even exist in popular usage at the time. Edwards
retired in 1962, five years before the publication of S. E. Hinton's
The Outsiders, the first YA novel, and so during most of her career Margaret Edwards was essentially playing the game without
a ball—without the stable of great young adult writers and teen-
appealing covers and jacket copy that are so essential to YA library
services today.

It is to her credit that the reading list in the second edition of
Fair Garden (1974) includes a few of the landmark books that came
to be called "the new realism"—*The Outsiders, Go Ask Alice*, Paul
Zindel's *My Darling, My Hamburger*, and *The Pigman*. Still, most
of the twenty young adult books she chose for a list of ninety titles
are "junior novels," an earlier type of teen reading characterized by
flat characters and saccharine plots. Edwards's dismissive attitude
toward young adult literature and her tendency to regard the whole
genre as worthwhile only as stepping stones is revealed by a heading in her bibliography: "Useful Titles for Transferring the Reader
to Adult Books."

The Alex Award, it seems to me, by putting a primary emphasis
on adult books, reverts to this old attitude and inherently diminishes
the value of young adult books. *Horn Book* editor Roger Sutton also
muses on the implications of adult books for YAs in his July/August
1998 editorial, "Nudging Them out of the Nest." Although he does
say that "we've gone beyond the idea of YA lit as 'transitional reading,'" his title and the phrase "teens do want to move on" betray a
subtle bias toward adult books as somehow better. Cynics may be
quick to point out that I, as a person who makes her living as a flea
on the back of YA lit, will naturally leap to oppose any development
that seems to lessen the importance of that genre. This is true. But
my concern goes beyond self-interest to the welfare of young adults
themselves.

In the past forty years we have seen the development of a mag-
nificent body of literature for teens—a literature too few of them

ever discover, much to our shame. Observers consistently report that most teens go straight from Beverly Cleary to John Grisham because they haven't a clue that any fiction more relevant to their lives exists. Or else they dismiss the genre as "babyish" because no one has shown them its range and depth. YAs ask for and want to read adult books, many librarians insist. But could that be because we have not done a good job of showing them how good YA lit is? To divert some of the energy toward adult books that we should devote to introducing kids to the riches of YA fiction seems to me to be a misguided waste of potential.

Currently there is only a small window of time—the years from eleven to sixteen—during which readers accept YA fiction without a disclaimer. Why waste any of the precious opportunity by promoting less relevant adult titles? They'll move on soon enough, but let's not push that transition until they've had time to savor Chris Crutcher's wisdom, Francesca Lia Block's audacity, Robert Cormier's dark complexities, Richard Peck's wit. Once a young person begins to read adult fiction, I am convinced that they seldom look back, and the chance is gone forever.

Airing these ideas on yalsa-bk, ALA's young adult literature listserv, I found some folks disagreed, maintaining that young people go back and forth in their reading levels. "I know kids (and have been one) who bounce from the Bobbsey Twins to *The Caine Mutiny* and back again without turning a hair," said Chapple Langemack of King County Library System, Washington. Are adult novels actually the kiss of death for YA reading? I asked two YA informants on the listserv, Matt Loy and Adam Balutis. Both are articulate and well-read enthusiasts of YA fiction, Matt being a passionate fantasy fan and Adam claiming divine status for Rob Thomas.

"Once other kids go to adult, they're not coming back," said Matt, although in his own reading life, he had gone straight from children's to adult books and has only recently come back to explore YA. But Matt also was adamant in his scorn for the Alex Award list ("total exclusion of fantasy") and his conviction that "it encourages kids to skip young adult books." Adam was more measured in his judgment. "I don't think there's anything special about adult fiction that takes away from the enjoyment of YA fiction," he posted. "I don't think you ever stop loving YA literature. I just think you stop wanting to *look like* you love YA literature. It's a pride issue."

YA lit expert and anthologist Don Gallo felt I was making too much fuss. "Kids don't read award lists," he wrote. "They just pick up books that sound good to them, whether they are about adults or kids. . . . Best Books lists and the like are for librarians. I don't think anybody else pays much attention to them, especially teenagers." I reminded him that the lists have a powerful influence on what books kids will be able to pick up in their libraries.

A paradox that emerged was the tendency of some librarians and teachers to reject "dark" or "cutting edge" books as "too adult" in content and theme, yet welcome adult books for YAs with open arms. The fact that a YA book has "the literary depth and thematic richness of better adult books, in a form and with a subject that could speak directly to teenagers" should be in its favor, wrote Henry Holt editor Marc Aronson.

The message is clear. There is no need to go searching for adult books for teens, but there is a need to make the feast of YA fiction appetizing to young adults by giving it an adult flavor, as many YA advocates have suggested recently. One way the Alex Award could be parlayed to dignify young adult literature would be to use its existence as a reason to limit YALSA's Best Books list to titles published for YAs, leaving the recognition of adult books to Alex.

Another strategy for making fine YA fiction more visible would be the much-discussed establishment of an annual award for best YA novel, especially if it is given a name, such as the Holden Caulfield Award, that would be evocative of its nature to the world at large as well as to librarians. I'm aware of the irony that *The Catcher in the Rye* was published for adults—but only because there was no concept of serious literature written for teens in 1951. I think that Holden would feel entirely at home in a YA novel. And if *Catcher had* been published as a young adult novel—as it most certainly would be today—would librarians now be urging teens to "move on" from that great work?

Blood on the Table
Looking at Best Booking

IN A REMOTE THIRD-FLOOR ROOM in the cavernous New Orleans convention center, fifteen people sit around a long table strewn with books, papers, coffee cups, boxes of chocolates, and bags of red licorice. This is the Best Books for Young Adults Committee of the American Library Association, a group appointed to produce the highly influential annual list of the most outstanding books for teens. I am here to watch them work, hoping to pinpoint some strengths and flaws in the official process, and also to enjoy vicarious participation in this twice-yearly book brouhaha.

A warm fellow feeling pervades the room, a sense of sharing a demanding job and a determination to do it well. Unlike committees I remember from my own four years of Best Book service, there are no signs of factions or personal antagonisms in this 2001 group. Although members often speak out passionately for their favorites, and other members often disagree vehemently, the situation is disarmed with cheerful anticipatory cries of "Blood on the table!" Like any group that has bonded in the face of shared difficulties, they have their own unofficial rules and catchphrases. Their refrain is "a *good* book, but not a *best* book." Nobody is allowed to say, "I really, really, really liked it!" So of course they say it at every opportunity, accompanied by muffled snickers.

Originally published in "The Sand in the Oyster," *Horn Book* (May/June 2002): 275–80.

Their comradeship nurtured by the enormous task they share, the Best Bookers are committed to read every nominated title and also to read widely to find more candidates. All but one or two of the members have come close to finishing all 233 books on this year's ballot, and Best Booker Diana Tixier Herald estimates that she has read five hundred books for this year's consideration. Although new Bookers are warned of this huge workload when they are appointed, the effect on one's personal life can be ruinous. Movies, family outings, Sunday leisure, television, vacations all must be put aside for reading, reading, and more reading. "When you're on Best Books, the committee *is* your life!" says member Diane Monnier. "If you miss a day, you're in trouble," agrees Jan Hoberecht.

Although there is a long waiting list of people who want to serve on the Best Books Committee, is it fair for the Young Adult Library Services Association of ALA to require such a huge personal sacrifice to produce the list? Is it even possible to bring sound critical judgment to every one of the 233 books? "After you've read so much you begin to lose the ability to tell if you're impatient with a book because the style is slow, or because there's pressure to move on to the next book," says member Cindy Dobrez. The rules allow an escape hatch: members who find the workload too heavy may resign after the first year of their three-year term. The only male in this year's group and the only member with a young child, Nick Buron, reluctantly plans to do just that. Although he has kept up with the reading for this year's vote and loves being on the committee, he was surprised to find just how incompatible the demands of his job as YA Coordinator for the Queens Borough Public Library and the needs of his three-year-old son were with the Best Books for Young Adults Committee's huge task. The one or two Bookers whose reading totals were low at ALA's Annual Conference in June earned the secret resentment of their fellow members, and their inability to vote on every title had a discernible effect on the early tallies. But by midwinter conference in New Orleans, every member had pulled up his or her socks and read at least 190 titles. "Reappointment [to a second or third year] is not automatic, but instead is based upon participation," read the official rules, but in actuality members who don't pull their weight usually earn no more than a private talk with the chair.

Could some way be found to reduce the size of the task? Perhaps separating the list into two—fiction and nonfiction—or splitting it laterally into books for middle school and older teens, or eliminating the amorphous category of adult titles and focusing solely on the discrete category of YA publishing? Or instituting a more stringent nomination procedure? Or reducing the size of the final list below the fifty to seventy-five titles that are now the official limit, but a restriction that is seldom honored by the list's compilers. Or doing away with the overlap nomination period from September to December of the previous year, which results in some books being considered twice? Or reducing the term of office to two years? Much to my surprise, every Booker I approached with such suggestions rejected them without hesitation and with a kind of pride in their own accomplishments in rising to the challenge. Nevertheless, the current committee's heroism is no guarantee that future committees will be as heroic.

Midwinter in New Orleans is the second time the group has come together, under the calm and efficient leadership of Chair Donna McMillen, to select the best books of 2001. At the meeting in June they had done some advance discussion and confessed publicly to the number of titles they had read so far—at which point an alarming pattern began to emerge. There are fifteen members on the committee and two non-voting participants—consultant Stephanie Zvirin (the "Books for Youth" editor of *Booklist* magazine) and an administrative assistant. A simple majority of nine is required to put a book on the final list, so a book with only eight readers, even if those readers are wildly enthusiastic, cannot be chosen. At the meeting in June many important novels did not have this quorum, especially in high page-count genres like fantasy, despite the presence of fantasy advocate Diana Herald. Particularly troublesome was the low readership for Phillip Pullman's *The Amber Spyglass*, which for an intelligent decision, required not only a knowledge of that very thick volume, but also of the two previous volumes in the trilogy. A related problem was the need for repeated careful readings of difficult novels like Chris Lynch's *Freewill* or Robert Cormier's *The Rag and Bone Shop*. Cindy Dobrez made an eloquent plea for a readership on these important books, and she and other members proselytized for their favorites by e-mail, so that by January every member had taken on the extra load and *The Amber Spyglass* had fifteen readers. But would this have happened without such a diligent advocate?

In New Orleans, the committee begins their twenty-five hours of meetings by going through the nomination list for a straw vote by show of hands, no comments allowed. The process lays down the battle lines and reveals some useful information about which titles are closely contested or need one or two more readers to be in contention. Much horse trading goes on after the voting, as members try to get their endangered favorites read overnight by their already bleary-eyed fellow Bookers. The fact that two members have not been able to come to the conference is a frustration in this electioneering process.

The next day the work begins in earnest, with systematic discussion of every title in nomination. Unlike ALA award committees such as the Printz and the Newbery, the Best Books Committee allows spectators and even gives them a chance to speak (albeit briefly) before each book is considered. Publishers, however, are forbidden to comment, although several of them drop in and out during the day to monitor the assessments of their own books—an indication of the importance of this list to the industry. Occasionally an author makes a discreet appearance but, like mystery writer Nancy Werlin, has the good taste to leave before his or her own book comes on the table.

The committee struggles with the perpetual YA dichotomy of quality versus popular appeal, and with a related pair of balances— their own preferences and those of teens. Nearly every analysis by a librarian is bolstered by teen opinions they have carefully collected on cards with the young adults' own reviews and precise scoring, using the model of *VOYA* magazine, of 1 to 5 for both quality and popularity. Yet love affairs with certain books are inevitable for dedicated readers like this committee, and emotions run high. "There's always one book that you'll lie across the table and scream for," confesses Diane Monnier, although she admits, "I don't have to love a book for it to be a best book for young adults." Nancy Henkel says stoutly, "I'm willing to vote 'yes' on a book I personally don't like." However, this is a list *for* teens, not *by* teens, and the Best Bookers are visibly aware of their professional responsibility to bring mature critical judgment to the selection. There is a tendency to be more lenient about standards of writing quality for books that are perceived as having a unique bibliotherapeutic function— "kids need to hear this"—and sometimes they pass over a title by reassuring one another that "Quick Picks will get this one." (Is an overlap with Quick Picks—a list chosen for appeal to reluctant readers—desirable? Or should there be some sort of communication during the selection process to keep the lists separate?) The day ends before the list is completed, and again there is lobbying for overnight reading.

Sunday afternoon is the day everyone looks forward to, the day when local teens are invited to share their book reactions with the committee. But Chair Donna McMillen is having problems with ALA's bureaucratic decree that the kids need badges and passes and multiple official forms. She and several members huddle together with worried looks, trying to sort out last-minute red tape. At last the kids file in and take their seats in the front rows, sixty-three excited and nervous teens who have each read at least ten books from the list in preparation for this day. After a warm welcome from the chair and a demonstration of what is needed ("No plot summaries, just tell us how you felt about the book") they are invited to stand up and hold forth. At first they are shy, but soon they warm up and begin to raise their hands eagerly as they share their pleasure—and their displeasure. Spectators crowd into the room to listen with respect and appreciation, even though the lack of microphones makes it difficult to hear. The teens' comments range from visceral reaction ("I laughed so hard I spit up") to serious critical assessment ("This character showed a lot of hubris"), and at the end the audience gives them a hearty standing ovation.

This section of the Best Books process is a popular event, and editor and writer Marc Aronson has suggested that it should be given wider visibility in an auditorium or even through nationwide video with input from teens across the country. But first the microphone problem needs to be solved, as well as the roadblocks ALA puts in the way of teen participation. Providing access to a broader range of books from the list would also be helpful, as the titles the teens read are limited to what is available in their local libraries. A new position, youth participation coordinator, has been created to work on these problems for this committee and others, and Diane Monnier has been appointed for next year.

When the kids have left, the committee settles down to finish their discussion, and late the next day they take one more straw vote before a last chance to recruit overnighters. The two missing members have sent their votes by proxy, but there is general dissatisfaction with this and mutters of "I'll bet they'd have voted differently if they'd heard the discussion!" The tally is 101 titles, a long way from the official maximum of seventy-five. Sacrifices will be necessary, the Best Bookers remind one another grimly.

At last the day of the final vote comes, preceded by a "pleading period" during which each member makes a fervent case for a book he or she strongly feels is important, and suggests a book to drop. A mood of solemnity pervades the room as the chair calls for decorum during the voting—"no hooting or sighing." And for the most part the observers comply, although when Louise Rennison's *On the Bright Side, I'm Now the Girlfriend of a Sex God* goes down in flames 2–13, there are mutters of "ten thousand teenage girls will be furious!" The final total is eighty-four, within hailing distance of the official number. There are thirteen unanimous titles.

The Bookers' final selection task is the top ten titles, done quickly by a written ballot. Six of these are also unanimous choices on the larger list: *The Sisterhood of the Traveling Pants* by Ann

Brashares, *Whale Talk* by Chris Crutcher, *Breathing Underwater* by Alex Flinn, *Damage* by A. M. Jenkins, *The Land* by Mildred D. Taylor, and *True Believer* by Virginia Euwer Wolff. The Printz winner, *A Step from Heaven* by An Na, is not among either of these highest choices, although it is selected for the general list. The committee winds down to compose annotations; there are hugs and congratulations, and the 2002 Best Books for Young Adults list goes out into the world to influence writing and publishing careers, shape library collections, and point the way to great reading for teens. And what will the retiring members do next? "I have a huge list of things I'm going to read now," beams Diane Monnier.

Prizes and Paradoxes

UPSTAIRS AT THE HOLLYWOOD PUBLIC LIBRARY in the 1940s, just inside the entrance to the children's room, there was a display that appeared at the beginning of summer every year. "Newbery Awards!" the sign proclaimed, on a table where gold medal–emblazoned books were lined up, the newly chosen winner right in front. I, a voracious reader, would make a big circle to avoid that table and go on to my own choices from the shelves. That gold seal was the kiss of death for me. *Johnny Tremain* had convinced me that all those books were deadly dull, and so I never read a Newbery winner again as a child.

Is the American Library Association's Printz Award, which has been touted as the YA Newbery, on its way to building such reader aversion? Recent impassioned controversy over the teen appeal of the last three winners of that award (*Postcards from No Man's Land* by Aidan Chambers, *A Step from Heaven* by An Na, and *Kit's Wilderness* by David Almond) have brought to the fore issues surrounding the eternal YA tussle between quality and popularity, as well as several other dichotomies and paradoxes that are inherent in young adult literature. These questions probably have no final answers, but it may still be useful to ask them, especially at this time of year, when the 2003 Printz winners are just being celebrated.

Originally published in "The Sand in the Oyster," *Horn Book* (July/August 2003): 501–5.

When the quality versus popularity debate is applied to the choices of the Printz committee, it must be remembered that the award is given exclusively for literary excellence, although the rules also say that only books designated by the publisher as YA are eligible. (To simplify the argument, this column focuses on fiction.) Teen appeal has been implicitly, if not explicitly, excluded from the deliberations by the committee's charge: "To select from the previous year's publications the best young adult book ('best' being defined solely in terms of literary merit)." The rules as they appear on the ALA website say they "hope the award will have a wide audience among readers from twelve to eighteen but popularity is not the criterion for this award." From this starting point, questions of whether a particular book will be read by teens are possibly irrelevant to judging its quality—or, regardless of the rules, possibly still central to evaluating its merit.

The debate as it has raged on yalsa-bk, ALA's listserv for the discussion of teen books, has focused on whether a book can be considered excellent, or even a legitimate example of a YA book, if it doesn't appeal to its intended audience. Tracey Firestone argued, "Having thought about this all week, I keep coming back to the same thought. . . . why would we expect 'popularity' to be an important aspect of a 'quality' work? How many 'quality' titles for adults are really popular with the average adult? Don't you think we're selling our teens short if we promote the idea that only books which are popular could express the highest quality of literature?" Ed Spicer went even further: "The point that a book is 'low quality if it does not appeal to the intended audience' can be thrown out the window the second even one YA reader says, 'Hey! This book is fabulous.'" Other yalsa-bkers acknowledged the importance of a literary award to increase respect and visibility for young adult literature, but some also argued for the importance of teen interest as a component of the Printz choice, even though, as Tracey Firestone reminded them, "We have Quick Picks & BBYA to select materials that the majority of our teens will read for pleasure."

Miriam Neiman shed light on the process by sharing her experiences as a former member of both the Printz Award Committee

and the Best Books for Young Adults Committee: "For the Printz
. . . I was much choosier in my reading. If a book had too many
flaws in plot, flat characterization, etc., I put it down and found
another book. . . . I'll tell you that our committee worked extremely
hard and communicated *a lot*, trying to nail down for ourselves what
'literary quality' is and how much popularity should figure in the
selection process. We worked our frelling tails off for a whole year,
and it was *much* more intense than BBYA. We also felt the pressure
from everyone else in the YA world." Because, as Jennifer Webb as-
sured the listserv: "Major awards have so much power over a book's
fate in children's literature. . . . The books with awards will be on
everyone's list; small collections will give them priority, and parents
scanning for a book for their child will be more likely to pick them
up, regardless of how suited they are to the reader."

Beyond this particular dialogue, there is also the factor of
whether the established criteria of the genre, the strictures and
parameters that have defined and shaped the form, should be
respected in judging a young adult book, an issue that comes peril-
ously close to Margaret Edwards's inflammatory remark, "Fiction
written especially for the teenager does not need to be judged by
the standards set up for adult novels." Certainly YA fiction *should*
be evaluated by the same standards as all literature: are the characters interesting and fully developed; is the plot believable and
absorbing; is the setting credibly presented; does the author have
something to say that matters? But judgment of a work of a particular genre should go beyond these usual standards to measure the
book against the accepted rules that define the genre's form.

In the case of young adult literature, these rules are closely
related to readability and hence teen appeal. It seems to me that
for a book to be considered YA, the protagonist must be a teenager;
there must be no extended introspective passages from an adult or
a child's point of view; the book must be plot driven with a minimum of description; it must give priority to immediacy and brevity,
and the point of view must have the limitations of an adolescent
perspective. Admittedly, a case can be made that this is a circular

argument: What young adults like is what YA lit is, which is what young adults like. But it is teen preferences that have shaped the genre through thirty years of natural selection, so these criteria are descriptive as well as prescriptive.

If a book violates even one of these rules, it is outside the parameters of the genre. Although it may be excellent literature, it is not *young adult* literature. Strikingly enough, at least two of the four Printz winners are not young adult novels when measured against these standards, regardless of other matters of quality or popularity. Perhaps these criteria would be a more accurate way for the Printz committee to determine eligibility of a book, rather than leaving the decision up to the publishers, whose age designations are sometimes more closely tuned to the teacher/librarian market possibilities than actual potential readership.

Other dichotomies inherent in YA literature also bear on this debate—honesty vs protectiveness, for example. Of course we as young adult advocates care about teens' welfare, so while we want YA writing to present life to them as it really is, at the same time there are realities that we would shield them from in their own interest. This impulse toward protectiveness on one end of the scale can motivate censorship attempts against mild expletives and sexual references, but at the opposite pole there are things that even the most liberal devotees of honesty might quail at revealing to teens— the most efficient way to commit suicide, for instance.

A related pair of imperatives results from the tension between realism and models of morality. Again, we want YA fiction to reflect the actualities of life, but we also have a deep-rooted preference that it present a picture of ideal ethical behavior and rewards as a guide for teens, at least by the end of the book, even if realism would dictate a less cheery outcome. (This one often comes into play in discussions of *The Chocolate War*.) Another duality is the pull between reading pleasure and didactic value: we want a book to be a good read, but also a "good-for-them" read. (I suspect that this explains many awards given to otherwise lackluster multicultural titles.) And yet one more balancing act is the tightrope that joins questions and answers: if a book raises too many unanswered life issues, we are annoyed, but if there are too many smug solutions, we are equally put off. All of us who judge and select books for teens teeter back and forth on these perplexities constantly, and the only way not to fall off is to balance in the middle.

The Printz committee members, despite mandate, risk falling on their faces if they ignore these dichotomies. Although there were dissenting voices, most of those who took part in the yalsa-bk debate felt that this year's winner, Aidan Chambers's *Postcards from No Man's Land*, would not have a wide teen readership. "I think it's for a select group of teens," said Jennifer Hubert Swan. "And just because it's for a select group doesn't mean that it shouldn't win an award for literary excellence." Miriam Neiman agreed that "the writing is indeed of high quality. But I think he was writing more for adults, not really for teens." Claire LeBlanc fumed,

> Some teachers or parents might look at this as the only thing their teens should be reading, and if I had been forced to read something like this when I was a teen, I would have steered clear of any other book with a Printz sticker on it. . . . It's fine to have a 'literary' award for YA lit, but if they keep picking stuff like this it won't mean anything to anybody. . . . College students would seem a more likely audience for the pseudo-intellectual dialogue that takes up one fourth of this book. I'm just disappointed that for the second (possibly third) year in a row, something that could garner such good publicity for YA lit is being squandered because the choice has such narrow appeal.

The previous year's winner also took its lumps when Ed Spicer said, "I can't imagine many of the teens I know picking up *A Step from Heaven* independently."

But he also remembered that the wind had blown in the other direction when Louise Rennison's *Angus, Thongs, and Full Frontal Snogging* had won a Printz honor in 2001. "More than one person said something along the lines of 'if this popular trash stuff can win, the quality of the award will mean nothing.' Poor committee members that get caught in the 'damned if you do, damned if you don't' middle!"

"I think time," he added, "the long haul of time, will do for the Printz the same thing that it has done for the Newbery. It will focus our attention on quality. It will get us to argue about quality. The general public will become more and more aware of the award and, just like the Newbery, some years will be better than others." And Linda Lundquist summed it up nicely. "We can disagree about the particular merits of one book over another, and its relative literary quality, but it would be a loss, I think, to give up the struggle to recognize outstanding literature for its own sake."

Bookstores and Libraries

Common Concerns

"BOOKSTORES AND LIBRARIES: Unless young adults become readers, neither of us is going to survive." Heads nodded around the table in the noisy meeting room in San Francisco as I spelled out our common concern about YA books and reading. Assembled here to talk about joining forces in this arena were three representatives from the bigger chain bookstores nationwide, a librarian from the largest urban public library, two independent booksellers, and one publisher who has been articulate about the need for new YA practice in libraries and bookstores, Marc Aronson of Henry Holt. As chair, I spoke from the perspective of both critic and former librarian. The library press, too, was represented at the table by two observers, Trevelyn Jones, book review editor of *School Library Journal*, and Cathi Dunn MacRae, newly appointed editor of *VOYA* magazine and former YA librarian. This company had come together as a task force of the Young Adult Library Services Association of the American Library Association to promote a liaison between YA librarians and booksellers. I had suggested this task force in response to the growing unease about the survival of quality YA literature and the loss of the older YA reader, as I believe that bookstores and libraries have many things to learn from each

Originally published in "The Sand in the Oyster," *Horn Book* (November/December 1997): 710–13.

other and that together they can form a powerful alliance for teen reading.

From the minute the participants sat down at the table, we were eager and curious to learn about one another's procedures and problems and were incredulous to find out what we didn't know about how things were done in the other camp. Talk bubbled out, leaping from subject to subject. I finally gave up on trying to impose an agenda and just let the conversation roll.

We began by exploring differences in our patterns of YA book selection. James Conlin, the national YA buyer from Borders, gave us a fascinating look at the inside workings of book buying for a megachain. Librarians at the table were surprised and heartened at his very evident dedication to quality YA books, although that dedication is by necessity tempered by the marketplace. Conlin exercises enormous power in that he makes all the decisions about YA titles, not only what books are bought, but also to which local stores across the country they are sent. By contrast, Los Angeles Public Library, like most public libraries, gives the local branch much autonomy in book selection, as Assistant YA Coordinator Albert Johnson explained.

Librarians were shocked to hear that Conlin selects from publishers' catalogs, a source that library schools teach should not be trusted for evaluation. The only reviews he uses are those in *Publishers Weekly*—a revelation that left us protesting until Marc Aronson pointed out that *PW* is one of the very few sources for pre-publication reviews. Librarians, we came to understand, are lucky to have the leisure to make decisions with the guidance of *VOYA*, *SLJ*, *Booklist*, *BCCB*, and *Horn Book*. By the time these reviews appear, sometimes months after publication, booksellers have already bought the book, evaluated its performance in stores, and made a final decision as to whether to continue to stock it. Nor is the literary analysis in these journals relevant to bookstore buyers, who are primarily looking for predictions of sales.

But common accord developed around the continuing puzzle of how to define "young adult" and where to shelve the books. Everyone agreed that the YA section should not be part of the children's area, but how to make that separation was a dilemma. Conlin and his colleague Barb McNally, national children's events coordinator for Borders, warned that they had a disastrous experience with plummeting sales when they moved a YA section into the adult department on a different floor from the children's books.

Cross-marketing—the practice of displaying a book in both adult and YA sections—has been touted as a partial solution for the demise of the YA hardcover. These booksellers found the idea less revolutionary than librarians and publishers seem to. McNally described their "Original Voices" promotion, a prominent monthly display in the front of the store that usually includes at least one YA author among the adult titles.

An important area of common cause was the activity that bookstores call "hand selling" and librarians think of as readers' advisory. We all agreed that this kind of personal attention is the key, but everyone had problems with how to keep knowledgeable staff available both at the information desk (or in the office) and on the floor. Hand selling, however, is the forte of the small independent bookstore. Independent bookseller Darlene Daniel described how, during the fourteen-year history of her bookstore, Pages, they have nurtured child readers who now, as young adults, trust them to recommend books.

Here Marc Aronson pointed out that librarians have resources that the bookselling community has not yet tapped into, such as the annual Best Books for Young Adults and other ALA lists, or magazines like *VOYA*. When it became apparent that the bookstore folks at the table didn't know what a "booktalk" was, the librarians leaped in with great excitement, all talking at once in their eagerness to describe the art of the booktalk and its power. As they spoke, the booksellers seemed to realize the potential of using the knowledge and skills of librarians.

On the other hand, the librarians were surprised to learn of the many programs and discussion groups already taking place in bookstores. Particularly astonishing was Community Relations Coordinator Jen Pfeffier's commitment to making her five San Francisco Barnes & Noble stores community resources, which includes giving weekly parties at an inner-city store for kids from the nearby housing projects, even though there is no immediate prospect of book sales.

However, LA Public's Albert Johnson pointed out that this situation was exceptional, because in most large cities there are no chain bookstores in the ghetto or the barrio, and so those kids who most need this kind of enrichment are not getting it.

At this point I felt a need to play devil's advocate by expressing the unspoken fears of librarians about the program activities of big bookstores—their sense that this is somehow trespassing. "It sounds like you guys are doing a *great* job of what we thought was our job—bringing kids in with all these programs and groups and hand selling. What I can foresee is young adult departments in libraries withering away if bookstores are doing a better job of what we thought we were doing." There was general disagreement with this, and everyone rushed in to explain what libraries provide that bookstores don't—a body of literature that includes a backlist and out-of-print titles, school materials, and homework and research help. Cathi MacRae expressed her conviction that "if you're a reader, you're in both bookstores and libraries—you go back and forth." Marc Aronson summed up the group's feelings by saying, "The rising tide lifts all boats. The more the YA reader comes front and center, the more they'll use both bookstores and libraries."

On this harmonious note, the group shared examples of bookstore/library cooperation. Visiting authors sometimes speak in both the library and the bookstore, benefiting both venues. The bookstore gets increased visibility for the author, and the library gets a free speaker that they would otherwise have to pay for. McNally affirmed that she was very eager to book YA authors and to share them with schools and libraries. MacRae described the summer reading programs in the Boulder, Colorado, libraries that have been supported by bookstores with publicity, sign-up help, and book discounts. She also discussed the award-winning and very elaborate banned books program organized by her young adult advisory group, which involved seamless bookstore/library cooperation. Book fairs have been held in bookstores, with the school librarians providing title selection, local authors as speakers, and advance booktalks, while the bookstore provides the location, a national author for parents' night, discounts, and all the ordering and bookkeeping. Librarians can also be invited to speak to parents' groups and to lead book discussions in bookstores, and bookstores can be asked to provide multiple copies at discount for library study groups.

The suggestions went on and on. Finally, the task force decided to put together a brochure, to be distributed to local libraries and bookstores, listing some of these ideas for cooperative ventures and explaining how we can work together to promote young adult reading. There is more to talk about, but a beginning has been made. Where there was formerly suspicion and competition, we have now taken the first steps toward affinity, understanding, and a strong united front.

Part Eight

SPIRITUAL MATTERS

Godsearch

Sᴇx, ᴘᴏʟɪᴛɪᴄs, ᴀɴᴅ ʀᴇʟɪɢɪᴏɴ are the three traditionally taboo subjects in polite American society—and in young adult literature, the greatest of these taboos is religion. Although the 1994 *Information Please Almanac* documents that 94 percent of Americans say they believe in God, and 95 percent of teenagers make that same assertion, the majority of "realistic" YA fiction projects a world in which both the personal and the corporate practice of religion are absent, except for the worst aspects of cults or fundamentalist sects.

The picture of American religious life that emerges from these books is unrecognizable. First, the stories take place in a society in which no one thinks about going to church on an ordinary Sunday—although a 1990 Gallup Poll indicated that in any given week 59 percent of Americans claim to have attended some sort of religious service. Occasionally one of these fictional families will make a ritual visit to a church on Christmas or Easter but as if they are going to a performance rather than participating in worship. Judy Blume and Norma Klein never show us a family celebrating the Jewish holidays, and very seldom do we see Robert Cormier's characters at Mass. Even in stories set in areas of the country where the presence of the church is pervasive—Appalachia, the South,

---

Originally published in "The Sand in the Oyster," *Horn Book* (September/October 1994): 619–23.

small towns in the Midwest Bible Belt—the characters are not involved in any religious institution unless a fundamentalist villain is
necessary to the plot. And beyond Sunday services, where in all YA
fiction are the church youth groups, the Hebrew or confirmation
classes, the Bible study meetings that are so much a part of middle-
class teenage American life? Where, too, is the mainstream liberal
Protestant or Catholic practice and sensibility?

And where are the good people acting out their faith in service
and love? Active members of a church, on the few occasions when
they appear in YA novels, are presented as despicable in direct
proportion to the degree of their involvement. "Religious people are
often grotesque," says Carolyn Cardmaker in M. E. Kerr's *Is That
You, Miss Blue?*—and most YA writers would seem to agree. Prime
examples can be found in Bette Greene's *The Drowning of Stephan
Jones* and M. E. Kerr's *What I Really Think of You*. In *Miriam's Well*
by Lois Ruby a teenage girl must suffer the pain of cancer without
medical help because of her church's fanatical beliefs. All of these
congregations act as a negative force in the plot, and their members
are small-minded, given to malicious gossip and meanness, and
often involved in hatemongering and censorship attempts—which,
it must be admitted, often provides material for some dramatic and
involving scenes. For instance, *Memoirs of a Bookbat* by Kathryn
Lasky pits Harper—a young girl who finds her salvation in books
from the public library—against the smug righteousness of her
parents, who are traveling agents for F.A.C.E. (Family Action for
Christian Education), a fundamentalist organization that special-
izes in fomenting censorship attacks in schools. The hate and racism implicit in her parents' ideas are brought home to Harper when
she finds a letter her little sister has written to "Jewdy Blume."

If the congregations are wicked, their leaders are even worse.
Only two good clergymen come to mind, both M. E. Kerr's cre-
ations: Carolyn's father, a humble Episcopalian priest, in *Is That
You, Miss Blue?* and Opal Ringer's devout Holy Roller father in
What I Really Think of You. More typical of YA fiction is the
hypocritical televangelists Kerr used in the last-named book and

in *Little Little*. Even more sinister is the charismatic but treacherous "Preacher Man" from Cynthia Rylant's *A Fine White Dust*, the homophobic ministers in *The Drowning of Stephan Jones*, the malicious Reverend LePage in *Memoirs of a Bookbat*, the cult leaders in *Miriam's Well*, and most malevolent of all, evil Brother Leon from Robert Cormier's *The Chocolate War*.

When the subject of religion comes up, parents in these books are either gullible fanatics or unbelievers who are obstacles to their child's Godseach. Pete's parents in *A Fine White Dust* are alarmed and embarrassed by his attraction to church attendance. It never occurs to the young seeker in *Are You There, God? It's Me, Margaret* to ask her nominally Christian mother and Jewish father for guidance in her search for a religious identity, and her mother actively opposes Margaret's wish to visit a Jewish temple. Flanders's father in *Miss Blue* puts a card with a mirror between the pages of her Bible as "a solution to your problems . . . all that you need." Such a God-denying self-focus strikes the title character in *Miriam's Well* as the ultimate blasphemy.

It seldom occurs to characters in YA fiction who are undergoing crises such as a friend's death, parents' divorce, illness, rape, or disfigurement to call on God for help. Only Judy Blume in *Are You There, God?* shows a character searching for answers through prayer. Behind the naïve façade of Margaret's prayer lies a great deal of theological sophistication, an example that is not lost on Harper in Lasky's *Memoirs of a Bookbat* when she prays, "Are you there, Judy?"

When young adults in fiction do search for God with diligence, it often turns out badly, with the loss of the young person's faith, although this is sometimes presented by the author as a desirable outcome. Pete's religious ardor in *A Fine White Dust* is cooled by the preacher's betrayal, for instance. Another example of lost faith can be found in Norma Howe's *God, The Universe, and Hot Fudge Sundaes*. Suffering from her younger sister's death, Alfie struggles to find spiritual meaning beyond her evangelical Christian mother's neurotic pieties. An older boyfriend influences her with his flip atheism—"believing anything on faith is illogical and stupid"—and in the end she rejoices to conclude that "perhaps I couldn't understand it because there was no explanation for it at all."

"Religious doubts are part of the maturation process," observes Alleen Pace Nilsen and Kenneth Donelson in *Literature for Today's Young Adults*. True, but how can teens be helped to confront those doubts when the whole question of faith in God is for the large part unacknowledged in the books they trust to explain their world to them? Religious inquiry is certainly a preoccupation almost as important as sex for many young people. But it is by nature a private matter. Flanders in *Miss Blue* says, "I had never admitted it to anyone, but I did believe in God. Was that being religious? I wasn't wearing out my knees at the side of my bed every night, but I did say my own version of prayers." Without many more such admissions, YA fiction is in danger of leaving each reader with the impression that he or she is the only one with such feelings.

To be sure, there are a few YA authors whose work reflects their own mature religious faith. Madeleine L'Engle comes immediately to mind, but also Robert Cormier and Katherine Paterson. Phyllis Reynolds Naylor has written for the Christian as well as the mainstream press, and in her Newbery Award–winning novel *Shiloh*, a young boy prays to Jesus for help in solving an ethical dilemma. M. E. Kerr has admitted to being extremely interested in things religious, although she is by her own definition an unbeliever. Chaim Potok, Malka Drucker, and Barbara Girion set their works in the Jewish tradition. And two brilliant novels have explored the inner landscape of Christian mysticism: *When We Were Saints* by Han Nolan, and *NIK: Now I Know* by Aidan Chambers.

But for the large part, the spiritual dimension remains unmentionable in young adult fiction. What accounts for this overwhelming secularity in even fine YA novels, novels that struggle mightily with ultimate issues but avoid ultimate answers? The fear of transgressing the boundary between church and state has been mentioned as an underlying cause, although certainly this is a misunderstanding of constitutional principles. A more realistic fear underlies the reluctance of publishers and writers to risk cutting into potential markets by offending readers with differing beliefs. However, YA fiction has dealt quite freely with the politics of abortion and the creation/evolution controversy, the two "Christian" issues most likely to offend certain segments of the population. "Authors are in that twilight zone of being afraid," suggests Alan Cuseo, a member of the Best Books for Young Adults Committee of the American Library Association and an active Episcopalian. Librarians, he proposes, have through bitter experience come to associate religion with censorship attempts, and thus find the whole subject suspect. Literature that "proselytizes" has long been excluded from library collections—but how are we to decide when a book fits that definition? "'Proselytize' doesn't apply to anything and everything that mentions religion," says Pamela Klipsch, an Illinois librarian who has done pioneering work in incorporating religious materials into public library YA collections.

The main point, of course, is that there are so few writers who are willing to talk to teenagers about God, even indirectly, or who have the religious literacy for the task. Of course, there are a number of paperback series published for YAs by the religious press. But the lack of religious awareness in mainstream adolescent literature is a statement that can be interpreted by teens to mean that these matters are not important or not part of other young people's thought. The distorted picture of the inner dialogue of young adults leaves a huge gap where God-consciousness, or at least Godsearch, might be.

Some of the ideas that are rushing to fill this gap in YA literature are pop concepts such as guardian angels, aliens as agents of salvation, visitors from beyond the grave, New Age pseudo-wisdom—and fantasy and horror. Fantasy literature can quite easily be interpreted as a metaphor for the spiritual search, with its dichotomy of good and evil and its heroic quest toward the possession of a miraculous object that determines the future of the world. The popularity of the genre with teens is no coincidence.

In many cases writers of young adult fiction have substituted other faces of the Ultimate: a profound respect for nature, a realization of universal love, or even the redeeming nature of a good friendship. Some of the best YA authors have used secular symbols to evoke spiritual experiences, as in the numinous scene in *Missing May* when the three mourners enter the West Virginia State Capitol and feel "embraced and even sort of expected"—which might be an accurate description of how it feels to come home to God, although author Cynthia Rylant doesn't say so. Perhaps the broadest perspective on this matter has come from Sue Tait, who is coordinator of young adult services at Seattle Public Library and also has a divinity degree. "The quest for the sacred," she writes, "informs much of young adult literature, although often under other names."

Wrestling with God

SIX YEARS AGO I FIRST BROACHED THE SUBJECT of the reluctance of young adult writers and publishers to deal with matters of religious faith ("Godsearch"). Now it is time to ask what progress, if any, has been made in slaying the taboo. What authors in the last year or so have had the conviction and the theological literacy to struggle with those spiritual questions that are so intensely private but so intensely troubling and important to teens? And what publishers (perhaps encouraged by the financial success of the evangelical Christian presses) have been willing to support these endeavors?

This search began to take shape as I was leafing through a new short story collection edited by Sandy Asher, *With All My Heart, With All My Mind.* The book showcases thirteen well-known YA authors, such as Sonia Levitin, Gloria Miklowitz, and Susan Beth Pfeffer, in stories about growing up Jewish, followed by brief interviews in which the authors talk about how they define and relate to their own Jewishness and how it has influenced their writing. Gloria Miklowitz reveals that her novel *Masada: The Last Fortress* was rejected by eight mainstream publishers ("we don't do well with Jewish subjects") before being accepted in 1998 by the liberal Christian publisher Eerdmans. Not all of these writers are religiously observant Jews, and for several, the important thing

Originally published in "The Sand in the Oyster," *Horn Book* (May/June 2000): 353–56.

is cultural identity and the link to the past through tradition. But most of them speak of how their writing grew through increasing connection with their spiritual roots. Reading through the collection, I found predictable but appropriate themes such as Holocaust remembrance, resistance to anti-Semitism, continuity with the past through ritual and tradition, and (of course) coming-of-age at the bar or bat mitzvah.

But near the end of the book I found a story that shed a sudden brilliant flash of light on the adolescent search for God. Carol Matas, in "Wrestling with Angels," uses as her metaphor that mysterious story from Genesis 32 in which Jacob wrestles all night long with a stranger—perhaps an angel, perhaps God Himself—and although he has been wounded in the encounter, he prevails and demands the blessing that will give him his name, identity, and purpose. In Matas's story, a young girl, Jaci, dreams that she is the one who struggles with the angel and wakes confused and troubled. She carries the dream with her to her Hebrew day school, where her friends are pressuring her to get something pierced and to go out with a boy she doesn't really like. She finds herself telling the dream to Isaac, a boy from the Orthodox tradition, and through his concern and an impassioned class discussion of the book of Job, she finally realizes that "my Judaism *could* mean something. Something practical. Something useful. A way to think about things. To make choices." We know that a spiritual journey has begun here. Although she cannot yet say that she believes in God ("What kind of God would let the Holocaust happen?"), she knows that the truth she has glimpsed inside herself is "maybe, for me, the essence of God. Mystery. And maybe this is the beginning of a very long wrestling match."

A way to make choices, but also a wrestling match. "We are meant to argue with God," says Isaac, and this may be a new thought to teens who have assumed that faith means accepting ultimate answers without the struggle and experience that makes them personal and real. There are hard questions to be asked, and fiction for teens that settles for easy answers does young seekers a serious disservice. Take, for instance, the sentimentality of Cynthia Rylant's *The Heavenly Village*, with its picture of a Hallmark-style afterlife, in which everybody who isn't ready to go to heaven gets to hang around in a cute little village until they've worked things out with good deeds. The last chapter of this theologically naïve story even borders on blasphemy, it seems to me, in its depiction of a God who humbly sneaks around after hours to take lessons from a master potter. (To be fair, this scene may have been intended as a metaphor, but it's one that the author has not sufficiently developed.)

A few other YA novels this year have done a more honest job of posing hard questions and tracing their characters' progress in the spiritual wrestling match. Sometimes such exploration can show up in surprising places, as in *The Adventures of Blue Avenger* by Norma Howe. In this delightful story, a confident but modest and ordinary boy decides to change his name to Blue Avenger. When he shows up at school in his flowing blue kaffiyeh made from a bath towel, everyone, including the beautiful girl he admires, is stunned and impressed, especially when he accomplishes a few mighty deeds through a combination of good luck and good sense. Blue has two preoccupations in life—achieving the perfect weepless lemon meringue and figuring out the question of free will versus fate. Luckily, his girlfriend shares his passion for the latter debate, and after much intricate discussion the ambiguous ending begs the question of self-determination. In the past Norma Howe's characters have been unabashedly atheistic in their conclusions, but in *Blue Avenger* we find them pondering the beginner's question of whether anybody is in charge around here.

In *Ordinary Miracles* by Stephanie Tolan, the two principals square off over what to call that power. Mark, the twin son of a minister, calls it God, plain and simple. But his mentor, Nobel laureate Colin Hendrick, believes that "whatever is in and behind and through all of it" is "a force or a field." ("After that, I wasn't about to bring up Jesus," thinks Mark.) As to the existence of the soul, Colin just laughs, even when he is dying of cancer. Mark's fervent prayers fail to save the scientist, and he must face the fact that his faith has been too simple and that, as his father says, "We don't know all the answers. . . . God's bigger than we are." This affecting portrayal of the painful cost of spiritual growth is marred by a trick ending—the old "if you dreamed it too, it must be true" ploy. A pity, because there is plenty here that would have held its own without such fabricated "proof."

In the 1994 column on this topic, I deplored the frequency with which the church and clergy were cast as villains in YA fiction and the lack of ordinary good people acting out their faith in love and good works. Recently there have been a few exceptions to that norm. In Heather Quarles's *A Door Near Here*, a little girl's desperate search for help from God, whom she visualizes as C. S. Lewis's lion Aslan, is recognized by a churchgoing teacher. He offers aid to the child and her teenage sister, and later, after the older girl's lack of trust has made her betray him with a false accusation that will end his career, he makes her a gift of an act of breathtaking forgiveness. In *Tribute to Another Dead Rock Star* by Randy Powell, fifteen-year-old Grady deliberately gets on the nerves of Vickie, his would-be stepmother. Although as a born-again Christian she is rigid in her demands, we can't help but admire a woman who is willing to open her home to this lippy kid. And in a spectacular break with past patterns, it is a priest in Paula Boock's *Dare Truth or Promise* who gives a young lesbian the strength to accept herself by counseling, "I think love comes from God. And so, to turn away from love, real love, it could be argued, is to turn away from God."

Apocalyptic themes have appeared in a number of books in this end-century time. The best is probably *Armageddon Summer* by Jane Yolen and Bruce Coville, in which a boy and a girl find their own separate spiritual paths leading away from the hilltop where their parents had been awaiting the end of the world. Sonia Levitin has produced two fine novels focusing on the spiritual strength of Jewish ritual: *The Singing Mountain* and *The Cure*.

Best of all in its evocation of the ineffable is a small miracle of a book, *Skellig* by David Almond. In this wondrous telling, two children discover a strange white-faced man lying against the back wall of a tumbledown garage, a man who is covered with spiderwebs and dead flies, who eats mice but loves takeout Chinese, and who (they discover when they lift him up to move him to a safe place) has crumpled wings under his shabby jacket. Who is this being—a madman, an owl-creature, the angel of death? As they befriend him he becomes stronger and more holy, and at last lifts them up in a circle dance of light. A strange and marvelous tale that is utterly successful in conveying a sense of the sacred, the Other.

Ten glowing examples from the last two years are encouraging, but not exactly an overwhelming trend. Out of the hundreds of YA novels published in the previous six years, there are perhaps a dozen more that have dared to tackle religious issues. Madeleine L'Engle, Robert Cormier, Katherine Paterson, Phyllis Reynolds Naylor, Bruce Brooks, and several other YA authors have written of spiritual struggle with honesty and integrity. As Carol Matas conveys in her short story, mystery is the beginning of a very long wrestling match with God, a lifelong encounter that starts in the teen years and has profound implications for life choices and the state of our world. We can rejoice that there are at least a few creators of young adult literature who are willing to acknowledge the existence of that central reality.

Part Nine

THE CRITIC'S LIFE

Shooting at the Library

IT WAS NIGHT, and the big reading room was dark and mysterious except for the island of warm light just beyond where I stood waiting. The crew tinkered with the camera and the sound equipment while I gave myself a silent pep talk. "Stand up straight," I thought sternly. "Shoulders back. Remember to smile." Under my new peacock green blouse (Marlo had said that blues and greens photographed best), I could feel the mike taped to my bra, right next to where my heart was pounding. Back in the shadows I could see the security guard leaning on the circulation desk, watching with interest. Overhead the carved ceiling and the upper balconies were lost in the gloom. Nancy gave my hair a last flick with the comb and stepped back.

"Roll 'em," called Lynn. My feet stepped into the lighted place and walked forward. My mouth smiled pleasantly, opened, and began to say the words. "Hello, I'm Patty Campbell, a former young adult librarian and author of *Sex Guides*. . . ." The rest of my mind was furiously busy giving orders. *Smile! Look at the red light on the camera! Here's your mark—stop! Turn the left shoulder forward! Smile!* I came to the end of the opening section—"*We* know we have something to offer—why don't *they* realize it." Finished. Thank heaven. "Great!" said Marlo. "Keep your chin down. Let's do

Originally published in *Top of the News*, spring 1988.

it again." And again. And again and again. We were shooting "The Facts of Love in the Library" for the American Library Association, and I was finding out that it takes not only imagination and a dedication to truth but also patient attention to the smallest detail to create a good video.

We very much wanted this to be a good video. Sexuality education in libraries is a subject I care about a lot. I've devoted many of my "YA Perplex" columns in the *Wilson Library Bulletin* to the topic, and I've written two books on sex ed materials. And now, with AIDS a sinister presence and teenage pregnancy becoming epidemic, it seemed more important than ever that libraries do a good job with it. But help was needed, as I well knew from the response to my workshops and speeches. As I said in a letter to Donna Kitta of ALA Video when we first began to consider the project, "Librarians are intensely aware of the urgent need for better sexuality information, but they are uncomfortable and uncertain as to how to start to improve their collections and services in this area." We wanted the video to reassure and encourage them, show them how to weed out the old stuff and choose the new, point out other resources such as pamphlets and film, offer tips on programming and be realistic about censorship attack but demonstrate that it wasn't as likely as they might think. We wanted a professionally produced piece that they would be proud to use as a training tool for library staff and trustees and at conferences and workshops. We wanted to do it in an upbeat, interesting way with a laugh here and there.

It had all started when former YA librarian and Kidstamps entrepreneur Larry Rakow came to visit. "I've got an old friend here in LA that you ought to meet," he said. "She's a terrific television producer, and I think the two of you could do good things together." So phone calls were made, and two weeks later Marlo Bendau and I met for a fashionable power breakfast at an unfashionable little café where the pancakes are excellent. I liked her immediately. She shared my passion for excellence and for things of the spirit, and she had won awards for her video work with teenagers. We made big plans and began work on a proposal.

One month later we had gotten enthusiastic approval from ALA Video's dynamic young head, Donna Kitta, and her selection board. It was time to write the script. I blocked. "I have no idea how to do this!" I wailed to Marlo. "Don't worry," she soothed. "Just write down what you want to communicate as if you were giving a speech." So I did, but it was awful—informative, fact-filled, but dull, dull, dull. Talking heads (*my* head) all the way. "Now we'll do the visuals," said Marlo. Little by little it began to come alive, as we discovered how to take one passage after another out of my mouth and put it into concrete form. I made up scenes in which teenagers conveyed the points I wanted to make and began to fall in love with this new way of writing.

It was very different from writing for the printed page. The ear is neither as subtle nor as quick with words as the eye. Concepts must be broken into numbered steps; sentences must be short declaratives beginning with the subject. Opening clauses and multiple adjectives are out, and figurative language won't work at all, as I found out when I tried to say, "A sex manual over ten years old is a map to a country that no longer exists."

"The eye will immediately begin to look for a literal map or landscape," Marlo explained. "It's a good sentence, but it's 'writerly.'" We changed the passage to "Discard all books over ten years old; they're hopelessly out of date." The discipline of paring my ideas down to the essential core was bracing, but I was worried by the apparent simplemindedness of the script that resulted. Again Marlo was the teacher. "The words are only one part of the communication," she explained. "In video the picture carries the subtleties and the emotional impact."

Another lesson for a writer accustomed to thinking of a finished piece as cast in stone: "Stay flexible," warned Marlo. "You have to be ready for serendipity on the shoot." In any case, much of the script had to be tentative at this point until we found out if Dr. Ruth would really do the introduction, located examples of library programs to tape, and knew what Judith Krug wanted to say about censorship. Before the video was done, we went through six versions of the script and were still tinkering and adjusting on the final day of postproduction. Version one got us a contract, and ALA Video was amendable to my request that the Young Adult Services Division get a percentage of royalties. Donna cheered us on from Chicago.

The next step was to find a place to shoot our video. I made up a list of good-looking public libraries in the Los Angeles area, and we spent days on the freeway traveling from one potential location to another. But something was wrong with every one—Glendale's bright red carpet might shimmer on camera; the county's light fixtures buzzed; South Pasadena was picturesque outside but dull inside; one Los Angeles Public branch looked tired and worn; another couldn't turn off a noisy air conditioner. And there were fees, permissions, insurance. One library required that we hire a security guard during shooting to make sure no patrons tripped over a cord; another demanded a fire marshal on standby if we were using lights. Nobody was willing to let us tape after hours. Even shooting on the sidewalk meant getting permits and paying fees to the city. I was amazed that in this town where at least thirty television crews are on the streets on any given day, every public square inch seemed to be covered with a network of prohibitive red tape and expensive hassles. But at last, in Pasadena Public Library we found a beautiful, traditional Spanish building with a variety of exterior and interior spaces and an administration that was willing to smooth our way and make us welcome.

Now it was time to start casting. For much of the script I would be talking directly to librarians, but I wanted the kids to speak for themselves as much as possible. At first we had planned on just one teen narrator-host, perhaps a celebrity who would be cut-rate because we were so worthy (or she/he was pulling low ratings this season). But as I thought about it, I found that what I really wanted was a bunch of nice, ordinary kids of several different ethnic and social backgrounds who would tell us about the information they needed and how they felt about getting it from the library.

We decided to hold formal auditions. But where? The house Marlo shared with cameraman Lynn Rabren high in the Hollywood

Hills was too remote; my apartment was too small; rehearsal halls were wildly expensive. Then someone tipped us off to First Methodist Church of Hollywood ("very involved with the 'Industry'"), where we could rent an audition room for $15 an hour. Marlo arranged for a camera crew, and I called around to the drama coaches at Le Conte Junior High School and Hollywood High. "A paid job in a professional video? They'll be there!" they promised.

On the appointed day, there they were—a couple dozen of them, well scrubbed, respectful, and terribly, terribly earnest. Never had I seen teenagers so motivated. Marlo gave them scripts, and they scattered up and down the hall, muttering to themselves in corners over the two lines she had assigned. One by one, we called them in to stand in front of the camera, tell us something about themselves, and then act out the brief scene. Some of them were astonishingly good. Others had obviously just come along with a friend, and one poor girl would have burst into tears on the spot if it hadn't been for Marlo's kind and tactful coaching. But when we called them back in to do improvised scenes together, we knew we had at least five kids with real talent.

For a second round of auditions, we contacted agents. The contrast between these professionals and the amateurs we had auditioned earlier was striking. The kids from Le Conte and Hollywood High had studied their craft—they were actors. Many of the performers the agents sent us were either pretty faces used to adulation, who mouthed their lines with offensive adorableness, or, sadly, teens who had grown awkward and gawky with adolescence but still thought they were the cute little kids in the 8 × 10 glossies they handed us. The best actor was a fourteen-year-old who had suddenly spurted up to a height of six feet and was having trouble getting work because of it. We reluctantly passed him over; his height would make group scenes impossible to frame.

The next day we looked at all the audition tapes and made our choices. It was interesting to see that indefinable quality called *presence* manifesting itself. Certain kids would seem quite unremarkable until the signal to begin—then, the second they were "on," would suddenly blossom with genuine charm and appeal.

Others—some of them better-looking—simply did not project. It was obvious that the video camera is erratic about whom it chooses to love. With much difficulty, we picked eight, making up relationships in our imaginary gang. "Well, now, Jake, he's the younger kid who tags along, and Cherina is the smart-mouth. Elizabeth's bossy, and she and Dave are on the verge of going together. . . ."

We still lacked an Asian teenager to round out the group. The next night, at a young friend's class play, I saw a lovely Japanese girl, Kerry Higuchi, doing a brilliant monologue. Afterward, in the lobby I tapped her on the shoulder and discreetly handed her my card, not wanting to interrupt her excited chatter with her friends. I was brief and cryptic: "I'm doing a video. Call me tomorrow." As I walked away, I could hear her squeal. On the phone the next day I told her about the subject of the video and arranged for her to come to my apartment for a private audition. Not until she arrived with her mother and I saw the woman's grim, stony expression, did I realize my mistake. How would I feel about a mysterious someone who invited my daughter up to her apartment to talk about doing a video about sex? It took half an hour of earnest reassurance before Mrs. Higuchi even *began* to believe we were not child pornographers. After that, we were very careful to keep parents completely informed.

The pace picked up as we pulled it all together in preparation for our first day of shooting. We juggled dates and hours to avoid Pasadena Public Library's busy times, to work around Lynn's shooting schedule, and to take the kids out of school as little as possible. We held a meeting of the cast and gave the kids scripts, travel directions, ground rules, parent permission forms, and a pep talk. We interviewed UCLA students for the job of gofer and hired ponytailed anthropology major Michael Dwyer, who was willing to be our slave for peanuts and experience. Marlo made arrangements for the sound and makeup people, lunches, insurance, and so on. I had always wondered just what a producer did, and as I watched her handling hundreds of details, realized the answer is "everything necessary to make it happen."

On the day of the first shoot I pulled into the nearly empty library parking lot just after dawn, my van laden with boxes of sex ed books from my own collection. Inside, the reference room was a maze of lights and wires. Michael and sound technician Ned Hall were busy taping cords to the floor while Lynn set up his camera and Marlo rehearsed two of our boys, Dave and Jose, in a scene. Over and over they went through their lines. At first they were wooden and awkward, but each time, with Marlo's encouragement and correction, they got better and better, until the small drama began to come alive. Dave improvised a line that got a laugh; we kept it. Lynn began to videotape; watching the playback helped the boys to sharpen their performance. A problem in timing emerged: Jose was supposed to flip the pages of an antiquated sex manual in search of the passage he was to read. The seconds of page shuffling seemed endless on the monitor—television is a voraciously impatient medium. A discreetly placed paper clip solved the problem. Again and again and again they played the scene. I was amazed at their patience and tenacity. At last Marlo and Lynn agreed, "That's a take!" Jose and Dave slapped each other on the back and shook hands jubilantly. Then the camera was moved for a view through the shelves from behind, and they did the scene again from this new angle until it was once more a perfect take. The two versions would be intercut during editing to add visual interest to the scene.

"Making a movie is mostly waiting around" is an old Hollywood adage, equally true of video. The other kids began to arrive, settling in with books, magazines, and games for the long day. They seemed to enjoy getting to know each other, these nine kids from wildly different backgrounds and cultures. When they got too noisy, we sent them out on the patio. Our imaginary gang was becoming a reality.

More scenes were rehearsed, perfected, and taped. For me, it was totally absorbing to hear words I had written come alive in the mouths of actors. We had told the kids to change expressions that didn't feel natural to them, and they did, but only a little. "Jeez" became "hey"; "creepy" was shifted to "weird." Jake was embarrassed about having to say on camera that he wasn't yet ready for sex. "This isn't going to show in schools around here, is it?" he worried.

By then the library had opened, and patrons began to wander in. We had been afraid that our taping would draw a noisy crowd, but we had underestimated the Pasadena public's degree of sophistication. Only a few people stopped to watch for a minute or two, then went about their business. The box lunches arrived, and crew and actors took a much-needed break at the long tables on the patio while library patrons eyed us curiously to see if we were from a familiar sitcom. Lynn, who had just returned from a long, grueling shoot in New Orleans for CBS, lay down on the floor behind the shelves in the reference room and fell fast asleep instantly.

Since several of our young actors were good at improvisation, in the afternoon Marlo let them try their hands at interacting freely in a scene with Vicki Johnson, Pasadena YA librarian. She proved to be an unflappable trouper, even when Erica threw her the line, "Don't you have something that's easier to read?" Later, as the afternoon light grew rosy, everybody went out on the lawn to do close-ups for the opening monologues. I had been sent home to rest for my own session that night. When I returned at 5:00 p.m., all refreshed and ready to go, the kids were just leaving in a happy group, and the crew sprawled limply in the reference room. While dinner restored them, I went off with the cosmetician to be made up. Bad experiences with other television appearances had made me gun-shy about lights and face paint, but Marlo had insisted: "A good makeup person will just make you look good, not made up!" Nancy was reassuringly natural-looking herself, and as she worked on my face (a strangely disembodied feeling), I asked her for one golden tip. "I always tell everybody to throw away their eye shadow," she said. "Especially if it's blue or green."

It was freeing to have someone else responsible for the way I looked, I found when I appeared in front of the camera. At first I was tense about remembering my lines. (I had been memorizing them for weeks while I walked the dog and had made the surprising discovery that it is much harder to learn lines you have written yourself.) But soon I found that that little red light was a doorway to a personal rapport with viewers, and I happily lost myself in talking to them about how to make libraries better for young adults. It was midnight by the time we finished the last scene ("Ha, the martini shot!" exulted Ned). I was exhausted and very, very respectful of people who do this for a living.

We had scheduled two more shooting days, but they were two weeks in the future. The ALA Conference in San Francisco intervened: Donna came to LA beforehand, and we had a good time looking at the rushes. Meanwhile, Judith Krug of the ALA Office for Intellectual Freedom had agreed to share her expertise on camera and to help us find a censorship case involving a teen sex manual. But as I had suspected, such cases turned out to be rare. After a diligent search, the best OIF could do was an attack on *Show Me*, which was close enough. Ginnie Cooper, the head of Alameda County Library who had won that battle, agreed to tell about it. On the last day of the conference, Marlo and Lynn flew up to San Francisco to join Donna and me, and we arranged for a taping room. Both Krug and Cooper were articulate and poised before the camera, in spite of end-of-conference exhaustion.

Marlo and I had pooled our contacts and networks earlier and come up with several strategies for reaching Ruth Westheimer, but she turned out to be amazingly accessible. Marlo made the crucial phone call to her agent: "Would Dr. Ruth introduce our video?" Certainly—and no charge for such a good cause. So while Marlo and Donna flew off to New York to tape that delightful lady in her humble and cluttered office, I stayed home and kept the phone hot for hours trying to find examples of library programming around sexuality issues. But this was late June, and there was none: last winter—yes; next fall—sure. But now? Nothing. Finally I located a parent-teen discussion group led by Planned Parenthood for a Northern California library. Was it worth half a day's shooting to take a camera crew across the bay when we went to San Francisco? But wait—maybe local Planned Parenthood affiliates did the same kind of thing. A call to Pasadena Planned Parenthood revealed that they did and would be happy to set up a library-style program for us.

Now another complication had to be worked out. Because I felt that films and videos were important sex education resources, I wanted to include a clip from *Am I Normal?* New Day Films had courteously given permission. But the scene I wanted to use showed a young boy in a library desperately asking for "information on the male penis, please?" while the other patrons recoiled in shock. Had we gone too far for ALA? I checked with Donna. "No problem," said that stalwart lady. "I'll ask around, but *I* think it's funny."

By now we had most of our video on tape, and there were only a few scenes and some odds and ends left for the last two days of shooting. Again the long hours and the patient repetition for perfection. Watching them at work, my admiration grew for Marlo's creative direction and Lynn's imaginative camera work. They lifted my words off the paper and gave them wings. For instance, the matter of the closed case: we needed to indicate visually that this scene was in the past. Should we use rinky-dink piano music or perhaps bleed out the color to black and white in edit? Lynn did it quite simply and effectively with a single ray of dusty light across a cabinet door that swings shut with an ominous click. The staff of Pasadena Public Library also earned my gratitude, as they welcomed us every day in spite of our disruption of their routines and shelves.

As we worked together, a kind of camaraderie grew among the cast and crew that will be familiar to anyone who has as much as shifted scenery for a class play. Everybody began to get into the act. To make the library look busy in our after-hours sessions, Marlo, Michael, and Ned took turns sitting at the tables in the background, busily reading throughout those scenes as if they were patrons. When Planned Parenthood had trouble rounding up some parents and kids for a staged library program, we faked it with our audition photographer, her young houseguest, Kerry Higuchi, and my husband David (who had dropped by to watch the fun and found himself recruited to try looking Japanese as Kerry's father). On the last afternoon, we took all the kids outside to tape the "B-roll" (or background fill-in) for the closing credits. As they leaped and shouted with unquenchable exuberance in a Frisbee game, then stretched out on the lawn to giggle and talk in small confidential groups, it was plain that real friendships had developed among our gang, and it would be hard to say good-bye to these kids we had grown so fond of in these short but intensive days.

Now we had all our footage in the can, but it was still only raw material. A video or a film is really created in the edit, and so we switched into the next phase—postproduction. One day I went up to Marlo's house and read all my voice-over lines into Ned's microphone to exact, second-by-second specifications. Another day, after Marlo had chosen a postproduction house from the many clustered around Sunset and Vine, we met with a graphic designer to discuss the logo she would draw for us as "wallpaper" for certain display scenes. Later, we worked with the "graphics box" to photograph pamphlets and books against this background. With a technician, we made decisions about the Kyron—the typeface and spacing of the words that appear on the screen—and watched for typos as she set the text electronically. We had a magical session "in paintbox" with a technician who did amazing tricks with color and an electronic "paintbrush."

At home Marlo and I went over the tapes and chose the best version of each shot. Editing is the most expensive part of making a video. Acquiring an engineer and renting an editing room can cost as much as $500 an hour, and we were approaching the end of our budget. It was absolutely essential that we finish the project in the two sessions of edit that we had scheduled, so Marlo spent days and days at the TV screen with stopwatch in hand, making lists of the exact point to cut—the exact location on the reels of each scene.

Both of us were excited and nervous when we arrived for the first editing session at the postproduction house where we were becoming familiar faces to the receptionist. Night editing is cheaper, so it was 7:00 p.m. when the engineer tilted back in his big swivel chair and said, "Okay, fasten your seat belts—here we go!" He flipped some switches and pushed some buttons on the vast control panel spread out before him, and our familiar first scene rolled up on the bank of monitors overhead.

Marlo sat close by his elbow, clipboard in hand, while I watched from one of the comfortable spectators' couches and tried not to say anything dumb. It was thrilling to see the continuity of the piece beginning to take shape, but there were minute decisions at every point—even though Marlo had done so much careful homework. Should we bring up the red or the blue here? Will it clash with the background color in the next frame? Is the pace of this cut right? Shall we wipe or fade to the next scene? When the phone rang to announce dinner, we were ready for a break from the fierce attention to detail. In the kitchen, where an ample buffet was spread out for everybody who was working that night, it was fascinating to eavesdrop on industry gossip. It was rumored that rock star Prince had just dropped in for a session—our young graphics artist was all atwitter. But the clock was ticking, and we were soon back in the dark editing room. When we left at 3:00 a.m., we were well ahead of our self-imposed schedule.

The next night I was very aware that this was the last time we would work together on this video. As scene was linked to scene, we began to feel a delicious glow of accomplishment. The kids were especially delightful in their naturalness. Hope grew that what we had created might really make a small difference in the world. Later I would go through a period of seeing only its flaws, but for now I was in love with our video. Lynn had come in to see the last moment of edit. Just as we made the final decision, there was a loud pop; grinning, he produced from under the coffee table an overflowing bottle of champagne and four glasses. As the credits rolled, we toasted "The Facts of Love in the Library."

Visiting Francesca

DRIVING NORTH ON FAIRFAX IN MY OLD VW VAN, I pass the farmers' market, where I sold melons and figs when I was in college and where Weetzie Bat bought plastic palm tree wallets and toy tomahawks. Up the street is the silent movie house, with posters of Charlie Chaplin looking like My Secret Agent Lover Man, and Canter's, where I adore the hot pastrami on rye but Weetzie prefers the potato knishes. A little farther on, the street is lined with Jewish bakeries, falafel restaurants, and strange dark shops like the place where Witch Baby found the globe lamp. I turn a corner, find the address I am looking for, and park under the branches of the double pink oleanders that line the curb. Across the street is a witch's house with a roof like spilled silly sand.

This is Francesca Lia Block's Los Angeles—and mine. A native Angeleno, I fled my hometown three years ago, driven out by the darkness that is the flip side of Shangri-LA. But now I am back for a day, seeing it all through Weetzie's pink Harlequin sunglasses, and it looks good. I've come to meet the author of *Weetzie Bat*, *Witch Baby*, and *Cherokee Bat and the Goat Guys* and to satisfy my curiosity about the person whom Michael Cart of the *Los Angeles Times* called "one of the most original writers in the last ten years." And

Originally published in "People Are Talking About . . . ," *Horn Book* (January/February 1993): 57–63.

to gather material to offer another perspective on her work from
that of Patrick Jones, who in his article in the November/December
1992 issue of the *Horn Book* referred to Block's world as "strange"
and "dreamlike."

It is a striking literary irony that Block's work is perceived as
fantasy. Although there are magical elements in her books and the
tone is pure fairy tale, I know of no other writer who has written so
accurately about the reality—or one of the many realities—of life
in this complex multicultural city. I know because I've been there
too. I grew up in the Hollywood hills, just one canyon over from the
neighborhood where Vixanne Wigg presided over the Jayne Mans-
field coven. When I was a child I could see the lighted Hollywood
sign from my bed at night, and I know what a feat it was for Weetzie
and My Secret Agent Lover Man to climb up there with real wine-
glasses in their backpack, because I've done just that. I used to live
at Venice Beach, where Duck and Dirk and my surfer son occasionally slept on the picnic tables on the sand. Three of my children
were born at the Kaiser on Sunset, where Brandy Lynn gave birth
to Weetzie and where Weetzie gave birth to Cherokee. As Charlie
Bat did, I took my children to Kiddieland when they were little,
and my parents took me to the Tick Tock Tea Room when I was
little. As a child I roamed the wild hills and canyons that are in the
midst of the city and occasionally saw a holy man like Coyote living in a shack on a mountaintop. Like Weetzie's family, I've hosted
parties in the backyard under twinkling trees where the table was
decorated with Guatemalan fabric and roses in juice jars, and the
food was a reasonable facsimile of vegetable love-rice and Jamaican
plantain pie, depending on the ethnic propensities of the guests.
Weetzie and Brandy Lynn and Duck and Dirk and Darlene are all,
with a change of names, people I've known.

Will I recognize Francesca Lia Block, too, I wonder as I ring the
bell? The door is opened by a tall, slim young woman with long dark
hair who welcomes me in. At first glance I think the house is unoc-
cupied because it is so bare; then I recognize the simplicity as art. A
few pieces of furniture hold single items of fine pottery or sculpture,
and one tall cabinet is topped with a pair of antlers. A far cry from

Weetzie's house strewn with "beads and feathers, and white Christmas lights, and dried roses." We sit on a pale pink sofa, and she offers me iced pink peppermint tea in a handblown Mexican glass.

Francesca Lia Block is definitely not Weetzie Bat, I decide—a conviction that is only a little shaken when she explains that this house belongs to her brother, an actor. Perhaps Witch Baby? True, she has long tilty eyes and is wearing black cowboy boots, but her smooth, dark brown hair has no tangles, and her manner is serene and elegant. As we begin to talk, I notice that over her simple jeans and T-shirt she is wearing the exquisite pink-and-gray silk jacket made from antique kimonos that Weetzie bought after the success of their first film. I admire the silver charms on her necklace, and she names them for me: a tiny coral rose and a miniature bureau with a real mirror that her father brought her from Florence, a little silver hand from her best friend.

She grew up in Los Angeles, of course, in this very neighborhood, and then just over the hills in the San Fernando Valley in her teen years, where she went to North Hollywood High. Her father, a renowned painter, and her mother, a poet, nurtured her talent from the beginning. "I always did write, as far back as I have memories," she says. Her parents read to her a lot—"there were always books"—and encouraged her work. In school she was in gifted programs and developed a circle of close like-minded friends, with whom she played imaginative games in which they made up magic lands. She remembers her childhood as "very peaceful," although in adolescence she had "a couple of really bad years."

In high school she and her friends were enchanted with Hollywood. In a recent article in the *Los Angeles Times Book Review* she describes how they used to drive through Laurel Canyon in a vintage blue Mustang convertible. On one of these trips they passed "a punk princess with spiky bleached hair, a very pink 50s prom dress, and cowboy boots" with her thumb in the air. The image stayed in Block's mind as the spirit of Los Angeles, and later, when she spotted another blond pixie wearing big pink Harlequin glasses in a pink Pinto on the freeway, the license plate "WEETZIE" gave the image a name.

Block went on to study English literature at the University of California at Berkeley. There a poetry workshop led by Ron Loewinsohn and a class in the modernist poets taught by Jayne Walker solidified what Block was trying to do with "concrete imagery, yet very spare." She wrote a number of minimalist short stories under the guidance of Loewinsohn and did her thesis on Emily Dickinson and Hilda Doolittle. During this time of very intense reading and growth, she became nostalgic for Los Angeles and for her own consolation put together a little book about the punk princess, who had already been the subject of some stories and cartoons that Block had done in high school. "I didn't take it very seriously at the time," she remembers. "It felt so personal to me, and not like my more serious work."

But shortly after she graduated, a family friend sent a copy of the manuscript to Charlotte Zolotow of HarperCollins, who immediately recognized its quality and offered to publish it as a young adult novel. Block was thrilled at the prospect of working with the famous editor whose books had been an important part of her childhood. "*Mr. Rabbit and the Lovely Present* is like one of my top ten books ever!" she enthuses. *Weetzie Bat* was published just as she wrote it; *Witch Baby* needed more editorial work. Like the character, "it was tangly." Since the publication of *Cherokee Bat and the Goat Guys*, she has been at work on a fourth book about Weetzie's family, *In Search of Angel Juan*. An adult book, *Ecstasia*, is forthcoming in May. Although the story, like *Cherokee Bat*, is about a group of young people who form a band, it is, as Block explains, "very, very different. The first part is based on Orpheus, the second part on Persephone, and it has a lot to do with the idea of aging and how the world responds to that."

Thinking of Patrick Jones's rueful report that many librarians are put off by what they perceive as the strangeness of Block's ambiance, I ask, "Why do you think people who haven't lived in Los Angeles see it as so unreal, not just your books, but the whole LA experience?" "Well," she muses, "I haven't had experience with a lot of other places, so in a way I take it for granted, but I think that what is reality for us here may just be very foreign to them."

But why should that be? Many novels are set in New York, and while readers in other parts of the country notice that it is not their reality, they are willing to accept it as a valid or even enviable way to live. No one thinks those books are strange or labels them as depicting "an alternative lifestyle" because the characters ride to work on the subway or shop at Bloomingdale's or live in apartments with doormen. Why should the second largest city in the United States be perceived so differently?

It is doubly puzzling considering that America sees mostly Los Angeles every night on television. But the downtown of *L.A. Law* is a very different place from the Los Angeles that Francesca Lia Block celebrates. The secret neighborhoods of LA and the people who really live there are invisible to television and to most visitors to the city. Weetzie's LA is made up of Hollywood and the Beverly-Fairfax district, the canyons, especially Laurel and Beachwood, Venice Beach, and Silverlake—areas that are geographically widely separated but culturally contiguous. Block is documenting a very particular time and place, and she has got it exactly right. Far from being subcultural, this setting is upper middle class—a fact that Block admits but finds uncomfortable. As Jones noted, Weetzie and her family have unlimited time and money for their happy pursuits and pretty toys—although they would most certainly reject his adjective *materialistic* as descriptive of their attitude toward them.

Block's strong sense of style pins down "the time that we're upon." Images are very important to her—a fact that she feels stems from the influence of her artist father—and she uses not only pictures, but smells and textures and tastes to evoke mood, place, and character with great economy. As a minimalist, she is a master of the single, telling detail—Brandy Lynn's gold mules with clusters of fake fruit over the toes, for instance. Her bent for poetry suffuses her style, as in the tender scene of the return of My Secret Agent Lover Man, where the sweetness of the couple's loving forgiveness is symbolized by the morning light on the flowers heaped on Weetzie's bed.

More fallout from Block's background in poetry is her sure feel for rhythm, as in phrases like "the singing trees and the early traffic,"

or "what time are we upon and where do I belong?" So I was not
surprised to hear her talk about her lifelong love of dance. She is currently taking classes in ballet and in modern and Brazilian dance and
has studied African dance. The three books have several cathartic
celebrations where the whole company, even the puppies, get up
and "toss their heads, stamp their feet, shake their hips, and begin
to dance."

An element in Block's work that is often overlooked is the humor stemming from the collision of the fairy tale and the real world.
Perhaps the best example is Weetzie's attempt to cure My Secret
Agent Lover Man of the effects of the witch's curse by giving him
megadoses of vitamin C and putting on videos of cartoons. The in-
congruities resulting from the ethnic and racial mix of LA are also
amusing—Valentine and Ping's lunch of noodles and coconut milk
shakes, for instance.

Block's satirical ear for voices is keen. She is too good a writer to
fall into the easy trap of producing a gloss of currency with popular
slang. Nothing dates a book faster, as any young adult specialist
is well aware. Phrases like *clutch pig* and *lanky lizard* are not real
"LA slanguage," as Jones assumes, but words coined by Block and
her friends and used as tags for characters. But she does capture
the way particular kinds of people talk, and the type of things they
say—the punk, the aging starlet, the beach ex-hippie, the surfer.
Duck, after all, never refers to anything as *gnarly*, but his voice is
no less authentic for that.

Under this dazzling stylistic surface are stories that wrestle with
the hard facts of pain and evil. As everyone who watched the recent
LA riots knows, terrible things can happen in the city where it's
never winter and the jacaranda trees always bloom. Block is keenly
aware of the paradox of LA, "where it was hot and cool, glam and
slam, rich and trashy, devils and angels." This duality extends to her
characters. The darkness of Witch Baby, who tapes newspaper clip-
pings of dreadful happenings to her wall, and her father, My Secret
Agent Lover Man, who agonizes in the night over such things, is
contrasted with the lightness of blonde Weetzie's loving optimism
and Cherokee's potential as "White Dawn."

Block's most intriguing creation is Witch Baby—"who is not one of them." With snarls on her face and in her hair she roller-skates through a nightmare of loneliness, carrying the world's pain on her small shoulders. In her angry self-alienation she represents the powerful but unacceptable part of every teenager that skulks and watches and cares for nobody while caring for everybody. I ask Block about the meaning of Witch Baby's puzzling behavior at the beginning of *Cherokee Bat and the Goat Guys*, where she burrows into the mud as a seed. "In the sense of the earth and nature . . . Witch Baby is always kind of curling up—her toes curl and every-thing. At the same time she's going to blossom in a way; she's going to grow and change out of that. She's going to get wings, you know, so she's going to ascend."

Witch Baby is a raven, Cherokee is a deer, and Raphael is a dreaming obsidian elk. The atavistic animal elements in *Cherokee Bat* form a metaphor that resonates to the dawn of mythology. The man's head with antlers is one of the oldest human symbols. The horned and goat-legged god Pan, in his total detachment from any social or moral value, is the most ancient god in the Greek pan-theon. Dionysus and his accompanying goat-satyrs pursued the wild Bacchantes or Maenads, who gave themselves up to ecstatic states. More soberly, the Blackfoot Indians and other Native Americans revered the principle of acquiring power through identifying with the energies of certain animals.

"I've always had a thing about fauns and satyrs," says Block. "That human/animal split really fascinates me. My Dad would draw a lot of them and talk about them. He told me Greek myths for bedtime stories. The animal thing of this book, the idea of them coming into their sexuality and the wildness of it. . . ." The theme appears in the chapter titles: "Wings," "Haunches," "Horns," "Hooves." These are the totems that Cherokee begs from Coyote as costumes for the rock band that she, Witch Baby, Raphael, and Angel Juan have formed. Patrick Jones compares them to the gifts of the Wizard of Oz that bring wholeness to the characters, but this is a misunderstanding. In fact, these gifts bring power beyond the control of the recipients, power that almost destroys them. The

hooves, horns, and feathers are given for a price paid by both giver
and receiver, and in the end the gifts must be returned, sacrificed
for redemption.

Cherokee's initiation into the great adult secret of sex and the
fever of sensuality that consumes the two pairs of young lovers
ought to be the most uncomfortable aspect of Block's work to date
for those who are made nervous by such things. Although there are
no explicit descriptions of sex, Block has made the wildness of un-
controlled ecstasy very vivid—but also the nastiness and the perils.
As Patrick Jones observed, these are books about love and family.

But love is a dangerous angel in the nineties whose wings cast
a dark shadow over all three books—and over all young people's
lives. Block is acutely aware of "the AIDS thing. It's something so
huge—I just get overwhelmed. I mean, it's hard enough to be my
age dealing with it, but I try to imagine what it would be like to be a
teenager now—to be thirteen or fourteen, and to not only be afraid
of all the normal things, but AIDS, too." She feels that this sense
of encroaching darkness pervades her work. "People need help in
thinking about it," she says, and hopes that her books have provided
at least "one little tiny touch on that."

Francesca Lia Block's works have been referred to as "Mozar-
tean." There is a deliciousness of detail, a deceptive smallness and
lightness, a distilling of the style of a particular time and place,
and a serious contemplation of life and death under the sparkling
surface. Block is a brilliant addition to the canon of respected
young adult authors. Her readership may be small in Patrick Jones's
part of the country, but it is certainly large on the West Coast. I
do, however, agree heartily with Jones that "there are still lines to
cross in young adult literature" and that "the journey is well worth
it"—and that it would be a great shame if the extraordinary books
of Francesca Lia Block were kept from young people by even one
librarian's fear of the unfamiliar.

The Belly Dancing Critic

Ya habibi! At last it's happened. Someone has written a young adult novel about belly dancing. This is a happy event, but not because belly dancing is a hot item with adolescents. Indeed, the *danse du ventre* is a bit old hat these days, and teenagers never were very good at it, the movements demanding a certain *ripeness* on the part of the dancer. No, this reviewer rejoices because of the delicious appropriateness of *this* book coming under scrutiny in *this* column. Although in the past there have been at least two other librarian/belly dancers in Southern California and one publisher/belly dancer in New York, "The YA Perplex" is written by the only young adult literature critic in the English-speaking world who has a hidden past in the ancient art of *beledi*. So this month we present a technical review of *Also Known as Sadzia! The Belly Dancer!* by a reviewer also known as Houda the Belly Dancer.

The story, written by Merrill Joan Gerber, is a pleasant romp about a young girl who uses her involvement with belly dancing to free herself from her overwhelming mother. Sandy is sixteen, a nice Jewish girl with curly brown hair, sexy lips, and fat thighs. According to Mom, if she doesn't get thin she'll never snag a husband, much less a date to the senior prom. As an incentive Mom hangs

Originally published in "The Young Adult Perplex," *Wilson Library Bulletin* (January 1987): 62–63.

her wedding garter on Sandy's bedpost like a medieval skull on a pole. Sandy is annoyed but unconverted, and when her mother and her athletic best friend, Pam, drag Sandy to Thinnercize class at the rec center, she and Pam's flower child mother, Melody, escape at the first opportunity. Down the hall they discover a belly dance class, which is more Melody's style. Sandy is reluctant to join in until she spots Sumir, the handsome young drummer. After one class, Nefertiti, the glamorous teacher, pronounces Sandy a natural, and soon she is deeply involved both with the dance and with Sumir—who turns out to be a UCLA student named Sam Kosloff. Mom is outraged. "Is this woman teaching you the *strip-tease?*" she cries. But Sandy persists, egged on by Melody and by Mrs. Roshkov, the lively old lady who is teaching her Yiddish. "All mamas and their daughters become enemies before they become friends," Mrs. Roshkov comforts her. Sandy's relationship with Sumir heats up when she finds that he is not romantically involved with Nefertiti, as she had supposed. In the glow of his admiration and in her increasing skill in the dance, Sandy learns to like herself just as she is, and with the help of many practice sessions at his apartment she is soon a good enough dancer to bring down the house at a performance for the Temple Sisterhood. Mom, who has fought Sandy's nascent independence every step of the way, finally mellows when she learns that her daughter is a celebrity with the Sisterhood. Even when Sandy's date for the prom ends up as a performance at the dance, Mom manages to stay calm, bolstered by an improved marriage and an upcoming trip to Israel.

There are some valuable themes presented with a light hand here: the eternal conflict between mothers and daughters, the meaningless waste of energy in an obsession with appearances, the shallowness of traditional feminine values. But the heart of the matter, the part that really interests the author (and this critic) is the dance itself. The jacket flap informs us that Gerber "would like her readers to know that she does a first-rate shimmy and a fantastic Camel Walk." This is probably so. Gerber name-drops the hip lift, the shoulder roll, and the pelvic tilt at every opportunity, as well as the sitting cobra and the harem shimmy. But naming the names is not enough. Gerber needs understanding of how these individual movements combine into choreographic segments, and how the segments fit into a whole dance. There are many other lapses that betray her lack of any in-depth familiarity with the world of *beledi*.

For starters, let's look at the rhythms. A single belly dance may use several different rhythmic patterns and tempos in a traditional order. Gerber mentions only the *chefte telli*, and describes it incorrectly as "rather fast, almost a joyous rhythm." Actually, the *chefte telli* is deliberate and contemplative, occurring in the slow, sensuous middle section of the dance. When Sandy buys a pair of *zills*, or finger cymbals, she slips them on and immediately begins clicking them "rhythmically" to the complete approval of the drummer Sumir. No one ever mentions to her that the *zills* are not just clicked at random, but played, in precise and difficult rhythms, and that mastering these patterns and combining them with movement takes long practice. Nor are *zills* playable straight from the store counter—the flimsy elastic string must be replaced with a wider band before they will stay on. However, to Gerber's credit, she does get them on the right fingers. (Even though the fingers holding the veil in the cover illustration are not quite correct.)

A peculiar wrongness in the book is the fact that there is not an Arab in sight. Both Sumir and Nefertiti (alias Sam and Nellie) are fakes, as is Habibi, the woman who runs the belly dance costume shop. Even the *oud* player is blonde. In the Los Angeles area, where Gerber lives and presumably dances, there are heavy concentrations of Lebanese, Iraqi, Egyptian, Iranian, Armenian, and other Arabic and non-Arabic Middle Eastern people. While it is true that most of the dancers in this city are Americans, wherever there are professional belly dancers there is also a coterie of Arabic musicians, nightclub owners, restauranteurs, curio shopkeepers, and aficionados. Since Sumir is majoring in Middle Eastern studies at UCLA, one would think that he might be in contact with this ethnic café society.

Sumir is atypical in ways other than his lack of ethnic identity. He is eager to praise Sandy's dancing, admires Nefertiti, and considers himself her partner. In actuality, belly dance musicians are a self-focused lot, who usually think of themselves as the main attraction and the dancer as mere decoration. Drummers are the worst, being natural show-offs. I once heard a pair of musicians complaining to each other after a gig about the division of pay. "Allah! She got fifty dollars more than we did," snarled the *oudist*. "We had to play all evening, and all *she* did was dance a couple hours." Dancers soon learn to treat musicians with kid gloves. In Gerber's novel, Sandy drapes her veil over Sumir's drum during the dance, and he smiles his approval. Any belly dancer who was so injudicious in real life as to interfere with a musician at work would risk sudden death or at least a tirade of imaginative Arabic curses.

Nefertiti herself is another misconceived character, starting with her cornball name. Her behavior is wildly unprofessional. She comes to class in full costume, complete down to the jewel in her navel. Teaching a dance class is serious, sweaty work, and no real teacher would hamper herself with performance jewelry and chiffon in the studio. And a navel jewel must be glued in and later pried out, a process too painful to go through for a mere class session. What's more, Nefertiti even drives home bare-bellied. She shimmies instead of walking, enters the class dancing, does a rib cage isolation during conversations, burns incense in class, and generally carries on like a parody.

The class itself is also very strange. The students include an unworkable mixture of rank beginners and advanced dancers. Nefertiti's first lesson is the hip lift—the absolute basic—and then she immediately moves on to what she calls the Indian side-to-side head slide—a movement so eccentric and frustrating to learn that it is almost never used. There is no warm-up, no lesson plan, no gradual progression of difficulty. Nefertiti simply shouts out instructions over whatever rhythms the drummer chooses. And worst of all, she calls frequent breaks, interrupting the continuity of the class and letting her students' muscles get cold and stiff. On Sandy's first day in class, after the first set of hip lifts, Nefertiti decides that she is a natural, which is roughly equivalent to passing judgment on a ballet student after one round of pliés.

It is this last that is symptomatic of the worst distortion in the belly dance aspects of the book. For purposes of the plot it is necessary that Sandy be able to learn so fast that she outstrips her teacher and is ready for professional performance in three months. It wouldn't do for the reader to wait around for the two or three years that would realistically be needed for such a feat. Unfortunately, for Sandy to be such a quick study reinforces the popular misconception that *beledi* is a sort of "exotic dancing" that takes only a lot of nerve and a big chest. The subtleties of the veil and the *zills*, the discipline of intricate rhythms and the interplay of shifting moods—all are lost in this crude misunderstanding of the demanding art of the Middle Eastern dancer.

For example, after Sandy's second lesson, Sumir invites her to his apartment to practice. He asks her to improvise a *taxim*—the slow, deeply emotional section. "It's a rather inward dance, as if you're communing with yourself," he explains. But Sandy has never seen any belly dance performances in her sheltered middle-class life nor has she been taught any movements in her class that she could utilize in the improvisation. This is like being asked to make a speech on the spot in a foreign language in which you know only five words and have not an inkling of grammar or syntax. Nevertheless, plump, nonathletic Sandy does it, to Sumir's enthusiastic approval, even when he tells her, "Do a slow backbend and lower yourself to the floor." I once saw a dancer in Seattle do this particular trick at a fast tempo without proper preparation. She lay on the floor immobilized in agony, her skirts spread prettily around her, until the ambulance came and took her away.

Other critics not so dance-oriented might pounce on several embarrassingly naïve remarks about Arab-Jewish tensions or complain that as the book ends Sandy is evidently about to go to bed with Sumir after the prom, although no one has given a thought to contraception. But enough nitpicking. To subject such a slight work to so much analysis is certainly overkill. When all is said, *Sadzia* is an amusing story that has some good things to say, and this reviewer is grateful to Merrill Joan Gerber for providing the opportunity to hip lift Houda around the room one more time.

Reality and Fiction at the Reichenbach Falls

MEIRINGEN, SWITZERLAND—"To travel a thousand kilometers to come to a place where a fictional character died but didn't die—you have to be a little bit crazy," says my companion David with good-natured amusement, as he takes a sip from his very small, very expensive glass of beer.

We are in the Swiss Alps, and I am making a pilgrimage to the Reichenbach Falls, which, as every serious Sherlock Holmes fan knows, is where the great detective (almost) met his Maker in a tussle with the archcriminal Moriarty. Any Baker Street Irregular in the world would be ecstatic at the prospect of trading places with us, as we sit in the smoky Sherlock Holmes Pizzeria in Meiringen, a postcard-picturesque Swiss mountain village, and contemplate tomorrow's climb to the very spot at the top of the falls.

A passion for Holmesiana is acquired in the teen years and is never outgrown. The coziness of the sitting room at 221B Baker Street, the thrill of a client's step on the stair, the intricacies and puzzlement of the case, the breathless chase through the foggy London streets in a hansom cab—all this is enthralling on first reading but grows ever more dear and delicious with passing years. But I am having a hard time explaining this to David, who is not a fiction reader.

Originally published in "The Young Adult Perplex," *Wilson Library Bulletin* (November 1987): 66–67.

"Do you mean to say that not only did Sherlock Holmes not die here in actuality, he didn't die here in fiction either?" he asks incredulously. I have just finished reciting the "facts," wishing that I had a copy of "The Final Problem" to jog my memory on the details. As best I can recall, Holmes had set out to force a confrontation with Moriarty in order to halt the spread of the fiend's criminal empire. Moriarty fled across Europe with Holmes in hot pursuit and Watson trailing after. In Switzerland, at the Reichenbach Falls (for no logical reason except that Arthur Conan Doyle had been here on holiday and had chosen the spot as an appropriate place to end the life of his fictional hero), Moriarty was finally brought to bay. At the very top of the steep ravine, with the waters roaring just below their feet, the archdetective and the archcriminal met to decide, as all great stories must, the outcome of the battle between good and evil. As good Victorians, they faced off like gentlemen. Moriarty allowed Holmes time to write a last note to Watson. Then they rushed together on the edge of the cliff, grappling in a deathly struggle. This breathless moment is engraved in the hearts of Holmes fans and in a famous illustration—the wild mountain cleft by the plunging stream, the two figures locked together teetering on the very rim of the abyss, Moriarty's talons at Holmes's throat.

Well, as we learned much, much later, Moriarty went over the edge, but Holmes didn't. On that fateful day readers knew only that Watson came puffing up the path with the local constable in tow, to find that terse letter of farewell. The good doctor was heartbroken and so were Doyle's readers. Eventually the clamor of protest forced the author to revive his character in *The Return of Sherlock Holmes.* In the first story in that book, Holmes (in what has always seemed to me to be a singularly dirty trick) appears in disguise at the flat on Baker Street and then reveals himself to the flabbergasted Watson. After the doctor has recovered from his shock, anger, and joy, the Great Detective explains what really happened at the Reichenbach Falls. Moriarty had lunged, Holmes had sidestepped, and over the archcriminal went (thus freeing Doyle from the awkwardness of a protagonist guilty of murder). Then Holmes, knowing that Moriarty's henchmen were waiting in ambush on the path behind him and would hound him to the ends of the earth even if he gave them the slip for the moment, made a decision to disappear until a more propitious time by pretending to be dead. He watched from hiding as Watson read the dreadful note, and then Holmes went coolly down the other side of the mountain and into seclusion.

So he didn't die at the Reichenbach Falls, and as all fans know, he lives yet, on his bee farm in—is it Shropshire? Yet it is at this spot in Switzerland that the international association of the devoted chose to assemble to commemorate this year's hundredth anniversary of the Sherlock Holmes stories. Early in August they came here to Meiringen in droves to hold a ceremonial reenactment of the death struggle over the waterfall. They dressed as favorite characters, and afterward in their deerstalker caps and bustles they crowded the public rooms of the Adler Hotel (named, of course, for Irene) and the Sherlock Holmes Pizzeria to discuss the enigmatic possibilities of the case of the Giant Rat of Sumatra and Mrs. Hudson's recipe for devilled kidneys. The citizens of Meiringen watched stolidly from behind their cash registers. They are used to all kinds of madness associated with the tourist trade. They prefer to think of their village not as the deathplace of Sherlock Holmes, but as the birthplace of meringue, and this year held a commemoration of their own, which featured a giant forty-foot version of that delicacy.

Back in the Sherlock Holmes Pizzeria, David and I are still talking about the distinction between fiction and reality. "People come to historical places to commune with their own personal mythologies about those events that they believe went on there. What difference does it make if it really happened here or not?" I challenge him. "That has nothing to do with the story's importance to *me*."

"But fiction is *not* important," he insists. "Facts are what is important. Fiction is by definition merely entertainment."

"No, no, no!" I cry. "Fiction is important because it's a concentration of truth. Fiction—at least good fiction—is truer than true." This is an old discussion with us, and I know from experience that this particular phrase, which is so meaningful to me, cuts absolutely no ice with David. I struggle to make the point another way. "Look,"

I explain, "right now you're choosing to perceive only certain events among the millions that are going on in this room." I gesture at the dim rafters, the noisy jukebox, the red-checked tablecloths, the German tourists in lederhosen at the next table. "Then the way you'll remember those events is to link them together in a purposeful relationship—in other words, make them into a story. And it's the stories you tell yourself about the world and your own life that shape who you are and how you confront reality. And vice versa." I look at him hopefully and continue. "So story is events shaped into an interlocking cumulative sequence with a point. In other words—history. And does it really matter if the basis for the story is in the exterior world or in someone's head?"

I've gone too far, I know, overdone the argument. The whole thing begins to slide away from logic. But still I persist in feeling that the dividing line between fiction and nonfiction is not as sharp as Dewey would have us believe. There are places where the border blurs, and the Reichenbach Falls is one of them. We parry a bit more but only for fun. After a while we go off to our van in the forest and fall asleep to the sound of the river's rushing waters.

In the morning we are awakened by the metallic rattle of a relentless rain pounding on the roof. The village, with its charming chalets and winding streets, is deserted and drenched. Even the pink and red geraniums droop soggily from the second-story window boxes.

We follow the road signs to the foot of the falls. It's a pretty good waterfall, as these things go, even to the eyes of two Americans who have contemplated the waters of Yosemite Valley—fierce, loud, and very high. We can't see the summit from below where we stand in the parking lot huddled under our single umbrella. A red funicular car waits in its cage, but the ticket booth is dark and locked. A small monument bears the familiar profile with meerschaum pipe and deerstalker cap, but most of the area is dominated by a *Nervenklinik*. We search for the trail, squishing around in the rain, up side roads and behind buildings, to no avail. There is no one to ask except the people in the mental hospital, and the prospect of explaining in German to a Swiss psychiatrist why I want to climb a muddy mountain in the pouring rain is too formidable. We drive away sadly, my pilgrimage incomplete.

"Do you think Doyle lied about the path?" I wonder aloud.

"Why not?" says David, grinning. "He lied about everything else."

Ending the Perplex

"BEGIN AT THE BEGINNING," said the Red Queen to Alice, "and go on until you come to the end: then stop." Or, to quote a more recent authority, the editor of this journal: "Knowing how to end things is an art. Drawing something to a conclusion, whether it be a speech, love affair, or war, requires discipline and a sense of timing."

So with what I hope is a sufficient amount of both those qualities, I have decided that the right time has come to end my association with "The Young Adult Perplex." The first of these columns appeared in September 1978, and this one will be my last. During those ten years I estimate that I have read over 2,000 YA books—and this is quite enough for any lifetime.

There is a certain sense of alienation from the grown-up world that comes from hurling oneself wholeheartedly into the futile attempt to keep up with YA publishing. At first it was not so hard, when there were fewer books in the field. Up until recently I could toss off a couple of young adult novels a week, have time left over for some adult reading to feed my own soul, and still be able to name all the YA stories about mental retardation or the three best adolescent novels about fat girls with only a moment's reflection. But more and more I find that I am drowning in the ever-accelerating flood

Originally published in "The Young Adult Perplex," *Wilson Library Bulletin* (June 1988): 112–13.

of books for teens, with never a moment for John Fowles or Susan Sontag. To be the Compleat YA Authority nowadays takes someone who is totally involved eight to ten hours a day with teens, their lives, their problems, and their reading, and who is willing to sit down happily after dinner every night for four more hours of adolescent angst. There was a time when my life was this shape—but no longer.

In the beginning I lost my job. The Proposition 13 tax revolt was afoot in California, and an assistant coordinator of young adult services suddenly seemed superfluous to the administration of the Los Angeles Public Library. Oh, they were nice enough about it, offering me jobs in other departments at equal pay, but I had had two exciting years in the field as a young adult librarian, and five delightfully creative years in partnership with YA Coordinator Melvin Rosenberg learning the YA biz, and everything else seemed unbearably boring by comparison. In the mid-seventies I had written a series of YA columns for a startling feminist library magazine, *Booklegger*, in which the outrageous was not only allowed but de rigueur. On the basis of my work in those free-speaking pages, *Wilson Library Bulletin* associate editor Harriet Rosenfield invited me to join the *Bulletin* as its YA reviewer. At the same time Bowker had offered me a book contract. The door was open, and I stomped out and settled down to try to earn a precarious living for myself and my four children as a writer.

These were years of total YA immersion. My household consisted of three dogs and four teenagers and any of their friends who were on the road or mad at their mothers. On some days their sleeping bags completely covered the living room floor when I got up, and I had to step gingerly around the recumbent adolescent bodies to get to my morning coffee. Wacky, tacky Venice Beach offered a myriad of colorful ways for teenagers to mess up, and the judgment I brought to YA problem novels was often based on firsthand experience. The situation was excellent for book evaluation—if I wanted an opinion I left a book casually on the kitchen table and later cornered the teenager who had taken the bait. If nobody bit, that also told me what I needed to know.

Evenings I shut my bedroom door resolutely against the din of *Star Trek* on the TV and Santana on the stereo and read for Best Books—at least one book a night, every night. My four years on the YASD (now YALSA) Best Books for Young Adults Committee were a demanding discipline but very good for the column. It forced me to read broadly beyond personal preference and to think out my opinions carefully in the pages of the *Bulletin* because I knew I would have to defend them at the next American Library Association conference against expert opponents. After I had served my terms on Best Books, two of my own books were considered by the committee for the list (making me—as far as I know—the only person ever to have been both a member and a candidate). The experience was excruciating on each occasion, and it gave me insight into how very important to author and publisher those Best Book discussions had been.

The "Perplex" columns on sex education manuals served as spadework for the book for Bowker. When it was finished at last, I launched into a project that doubled the chaos component of my domestic arrangements. *Passing the Hat: Street Performers in America* began with my experience as a street dancer in Venice, and eventually it filled our house with Arabic musicians, jugglers, itinerant fiddlers and magicians, and even, for one memorable week, an entire string band. But publishing deadlines are implacable and so the Perplex got written, although occasionally a bit late. One Christmas season I wrote my editor a letter of explanation to accompany a tardy column. In one week we had all had Christmas, house guests, and the flu; my car broke down five times; my eldest son had a large, emotionally complicated wedding; a Hungarian drummer collapsed on my sofa for three days with blood poisoning; and an earthquake broke all the sewer pipes. "Forget the column," she said. "We'll publish the letter."

But teenagers grow up, which is their salvation and our sorrow. When they had all gone their separate ways, I rented out the house, got married, and set off for Europe to research a sequel to *Passing the Hat*, taking the Perplex with me. That year, and every year since,

I spent three months on the Continent following my nose to YA informants wherever we might be and then retreating to the folding table in our old VW van to type out a column on a tiny 1926 portable typewriter that we found at a flea market. Handing the finished Perplex over to the safekeeping of strange postal systems always made me a bit nervous, especially in Italy the year we heard that the postmaster had been fired for selling mail as scrap paper.

But the column always arrived safely in the Bronx at the WLB offices, and only twice have I failed to find any relevant YA matters to write about. Reaction to these European columns has been mixed: some librarians find them enjoyable but irrelevant, and others agree with me that it is important to measure ourselves against how it goes with YAs in Dubrovnik Public Library, at the Swedish birth control clinics, or under the thumb of the German censorship bureau.

General reader reaction to the Perplex over the years has been warm and supportive, and I am grateful to all the librarians who wrote me kind letters that let me know that my efforts were of some use out there. But, unfortunately, a journalistic axiom has it that praise is what they tell you in the halls, and criticism is what they put in letters to the editor. Readers have written to the magazine to correct my Parisian geography and my German capitalization and to pounce with heat when it seems to them that I have been insufficiently protective of teenage virginity and verbal innocence. To those readers, too, I am grateful for their desire to set things right.

So what comes next? My Perplex days have come to their proper end, and my place will be taken in the fall by a capable new YA columnist, Cathi Edgerton (now Cathi Dunn MacRae), a YA librarian who has gained national notice at ALA conferences for her ability to listen to the kids and make the rest of us sit up and pay attention to what they have said. As for myself, I want to go play with the grown-ups for a while, but I am not abandoning adolescent literature, only stepping back from the necessity of reading a coming-of-age novel every night. I will continue to take great pleasure in my work as general editor of the Twayne Young Adult

Author series and to write an occasional YA article or review for other journals. Nor am I leaving the *Wilson Library Bulletin*—in September I will launch a new column of criticism of the adult independent press, "Alternate Routes," which will be personal and free roaming and occasionally outrageous. Endings are beginnings, too, so good-bye, my dear teenagers and my dear YA librarians, and hello to new endeavors!

"Endings are beginnings" proved true after this column, with which, rather perversely, I have chosen to end this book. Afterward I settled down to rummaging through the output of the independent press for the outrageous, the outré, and the downright silly, fodder for my new assignment, "Alternate Routes" (later called "Outer Limits"), but in just five years, I was back on that wild YA ride—and I still am.

Appendix

━━━━━━━━━━━━○━━━━━━━━━━━━

Twayne's Young Adult Author Series

Presenting Robert Cormier by Patty Campbell. 1985, updated ed.
1989. Dell pbk. 1990.

Presenting M. E. Kerr by Alleen Pace Nilsen. 1986, updated ed.
1997. Dell pbk. 1990.

Presenting S. E. Hinton by Jay Daly. 1987, updated ed. 1989. Dell
pbk. 1989.

Presenting Norma Fox Mazer by Sally Holmes Holtze. 1987. Dell
pbk. 1989.

Presenting Rosa Guy by Jerrie Norris. 1988. Dell pbk. 1992.

Presenting Norma Klein by Allene Stuart Phy. 1988.

Presenting Paul Zindel by Jack Jacob Forman. 1988.

Presenting Richard Peck by Don Gallo. 1989. Dell pbk. (rev. ed.)
1993.

Presenting Sue Ellen Bridgers by Ted Hipple. 1990.

Presenting Judy Blume by Maryann N. Weidt. 1990.

Presenting Zibby Oneal by Susan P. Bloom and Cathryn M. Mercier. 1991.

Presenting Walter Dean Myers by Rudine Sims Bishop. 1991.

Presenting William Sleator by James E. Davis and Hazel K. Davis.
1992.

Presenting Young Adult Horror Fiction by Cosette Kies. 1992.

Presenting Lois Duncan by Cosette Kies. 1993.

Presenting Madeleine L'Engle by Donald R. Hettinga. 1993.
Presenting Laurence Yep by Dianne Johnson-Feelings. 1995.
Presenting Ouida Sebestyen by Virginia R. Monseau. 1995.
Presenting Paula Danziger by Kathleen Krull. 1995.
Presenting Robert Lipsyte by Michael Cart. 1995.
Presenting Cynthia Voigt by Suzanne Elizabeth Reid. 1995.
Presenting Gary Paulsen by Gary M. Salvner. 1996.
Presenting Lynn Hall by Susan Stan. 1996.
Presenting Harry Mazer by Arthea J. S. Reed. 1996.
Presenting Chris Crutcher by Terry Davis. 1997.
Presenting Avi by Susan P. Bloom and Cathryn M. Mercier. 1997.
Presenting Phyllis Reynolds Naylor by Lois Thomas Stover. 1997.
Presenting Kathryn Lasky by Joanne Brown. 1998.
Presenting Barbara Wersba by Elizabeth A. Poe. 1998.
Presenting Young Adult Science Fiction by Suzanne Elizabeth Reid. 1998.
Presenting Young Adult Fantasy Fiction by Cathi Dunn MacRae. 1998.
Presenting Mildred Taylor by Chris Crowe. 1999.

Subject Index

Author and Title *Index*

233

About the Author

Patty Campbell has been a librarian, teacher, writer, and critic specializing in books for young adults for almost forty years. From 1993 until 2007 she wrote "The Sand in the Oyster" for *Horn Book Magazine*, a column about controversial issues in young adult literature, and she continues to write articles and reviews for that journal. Her literary criticism has also been published in the *New York Times Book Review* and many other journals. Campbell is the author of seven books, most recently *Robert Cormier: Daring to Disturb the Universe* (2006) and *War Is . . . Soldiers, Survivors, and Storytellers Talk about War* (2008), coedited with Marc Aronson. She shaped and edited the series Twayne's Young Adult Authors, the precursor to her Scarecrow Studies in Young Adult Literature. She has taught adolescent literature at UCLA and has lectured on the subject for—among others—San Jose State University, Denver University, and the Bureau of Research and Development. As a librarian in the 1970s she was the assistant coordinator of Young Adult Services for Los Angeles Public Library. In 1989 Campbell was the recipient of the American Library Association's Grolier Award and in 2001 she won the ALAN Award from the Assembly on Adolescent Literature of the National Council of Teachers of English, both given for distinguished achievement with young people and books.

Breinigsville, PA USA
12 February 2010
232327BV00001B/2/P